BY WHAT AUTHORITY?

BY WHAT AUTHORITY?

A Primer on Scripture, the Magisterium, and the Sense of the Faithful

Richard R. Gaillardetz

LITURGICAL PRESS
Collegeville, Minnesota

www.litpress.org

7   8

ISBN 13: 978-0-8146-2872-0
ISBN 10: 0-8146-2872-9

Library of Congress Cataloging-in-Publication Data

Gaillardetz, Richard R., 1958–
   By what authority? : a primer on Scripture, the magisterium, and the sense of the faithful / Richard R. Gaillardetz.
      p. cm.
   Includes bibliographical references and index.
   ISBN 0-8146-2872-9 (alk. paper)
      1. Authority—Religious aspects—Catholic Church. 2. Catholic Church—Doctrines. I. Title.

BX1753.G25 2003
262'.8—dc21

2003051663

CONTENTS

PART THREE

THE AUTHORITY OF
THE BELIEVING COMMUNITY

To my son Andrew,
in gratitude for his humor and finely honed
sense of fairness—such wonderful gifts to our family.

ABBREVIATIONS

CD   The Second Vatican Council's Decree on the Pastoral Office of the Bishop [*Christus Dominus*]

DV   The Second Vatican Council's Dogmatic Constitution on Divine Revelation [*Dei Verbum*]

GS   The Second Vatican Council's Pastoral Constitution on the Church in the Modern World [*Gaudium et spes*]

LG   The Second Vatican Council's Dogmatic Constitution on the Church [*Lumen gentium*]

NA   The Second Vatican Council's Declaration on the Relation of the Church to Non-Christian Religions [*Nostra Aetate*]

SC   The Second Vatican Council's Constitution on the Sacred Liturgy [*Sacrosanctum concilium*]

UR   The Second Vatican Council's Decree on Ecumenism [*Unitatis redintegratio*]

UUS   Pope John Paul II's Encyclical on Ecumenism [*Ut Unum Sint*]

PREFACE

"By what authority do you do these things?" It was a question posed to Jesus by his critics on several occasions. He never gave them a direct answer. The question itself speaks to the very meaning of authority. In effect, what was being asked was, "who is the true author of your actions?" Jesus' entire life and ministry offered the only real answer to the question. God was the true Author of Jesus' life. His authority was grounded in his relationship to the one he dared address as "Abba."

The Church lives to proclaim the message of Jesus Christ, the Word of God. It too depends as well for its authority on God, the Author of life. The Church does not possess authority any more than Jesus possessed it. Indeed, authority is not really a possession at all. Authority names a quality of relationship. This explains one of the perennial dangers of any claim to authority in the Church. The danger lies in the mistaken notion that authority resides in persons (e.g., popes and bishops) or objects (e.g., the Bible). But this way of speaking of authority is misleading, for in the final analysis authority pertains to a relationship more than a person or object.

A person is only an authority to the extent that his or her authority is acknowledged by others. For example, as a professor, I can only function as an authority in the classroom to the extent that my students acknowledge that authority in me. If they choose to view me as a benighted idiot, I lose my authority in their eyes; I cease to be an authority for them. The authority is maintained in the character of our relationship. The same is true for religious authority. Where one might speak of the Bible, the creed or a pope as possessing authority, this authority in fact resides in the relationship between the community of faith and the Bible, the creed or the pope. True authority is always

maintained in a relationship between two realities, the one acknowledging the authority and the one manifesting that authority.

This book is about authority in the Church. In particular, the focus
will be on the exercise of authority as it is oriented toward Christian
belief, that is the authoritative relationships concerned with: the Bible,
tradition, popes and bishops, creeds and doctrine, theologians and all
the faithful. In an introductory book of this size it will be impossible
to consider those many questions regarding the exercise of authority
in church governance or in regard to the sacramental and liturgical
life of the Church.

Many of the sad divisions in Christianity have occurred because of
disagreements about both the appropriate sources of Christian authority and its proper exercise. Often the authority of Scripture has
been played off against the authority of tradition, or the authority of
church office (e.g., pope and bishops) against the authority of theologians or ordinary believers. A healthy Catholic view of authority will
try to avoid these oppositions and instead demonstrate how these various kinds of authorities inter-relate and support one another.

Each of the topics considered in this volume will be considered
within the context of the teaching of Vatican II. Held between 1962
and 1965, the Second Vatican Council effected a seismic shift in Catholic consciousness, unlike anything encountered since the sixteenth
century. The impact of the council lay not only in the sixteen documents that the bishops promulgated, but in the new frame of reference the council offered for considering Catholic faith today. This
new framework benefited from a series of new relationships being forged
where antagonisms had predominated. Once the rise of modern science and critical historical scholarship had been met with suspicion,
now the council called for a new respect for modern science and an
unprecedented openness to the fruit of historical scholarship. Where
clergy and laity were seen as two "ranks" in which the sole responsibility of the laity was to obey the clergy, the council called for their cooperation and affirmed the shared identity of all believers as the
Christifideles, the Christian faithful. Where the work of theologians
had been limited to explaining church teaching to the laity, now bishops and theologians were placed in common service to the Word of
God. Where the world was seen as dangerous, now the council saw
the workings of God's grace in the world and the possibility for respectful and fruitful dialogue between Church and world.

This new framework for understanding Catholicism did not repudiate the past in favor of novelty or relevance. It was the product of two principal forces at work in the council: the first was the determination to bring the Church up-to-date in areas where its faith and practice were no longer intelligible to the modern world. The second was the desire to return to the sources of Christianity in order to rediscover biblical and early church insights into the Christian life that had been neglected in modern Catholicism.

This book has been written in the spirit of Vatican II. This does not mean that the answer to every question we will consider can be found in the council documents; the council members themselves recognized that many questions and issues required further reflection and development. It does mean that the teaching of Vatican II will provide the immediate frame of reference for considering key questions regarding church authority.

The book is divided into three different sections. Part One looks at questions related to the authority of Scripture and tradition within Roman Catholicism. Catholics give Scripture a central place in the life of the Church, but many are confused about the authority of Scripture. All Christians believe the Bible is, in some sense, inspired, but they mean different things by this. We will look in more detail at different theories of biblical inspiration and will consider the difficult question of whether there can be errors in the Bible. A brief perusal of the Bible contents reveals that there are books included in the Catholic version that are not found in other versions of the Bible. Why? How exactly did this biblical canon, this definitive list of sacred texts, come into existence in the first place? Questions such as these will be explored in the early chapters. Finally we will explore some contemporary Catholic perspectives on the relationship between revelation, Scripture and tradition.

Part Two turns to the authority of those who teach in an official capacity within the Catholic Church, the pope and bishops. Catholics refer to the special teaching authority of the pope and bishops as the *magisterium*. This second section will explore the theological foundations of the magisterium and its diverse modes of exercise. Since not all church teachings bear the same authoritative weight, it will also be necessary to attend to the necessary gradations in the authority of church doctrine.

Finally, Part Three attends to a neglected topic, namely, the particular authority that ordinary believers and the entire believing community possess by virtue of their baptism. The Second Vatican Council addressed this in its consideration of the *sensus fidelium,* the "sense of the faithful." We will explore how the whole Christian community discerns the meaning and significance of the Word of God for today.

Traditionally, the authority of theologians has been related to the magisterium. Before Vatican II it was commonly held that the principal task of the theologian was to explain official church teaching. More and more today the work of the theologian has been related as well to the faith insight of the whole people of God. In this final section we will consider the changing role of the theologian as well as the sensitive issue concerning what happens when a person finds that they disagree with church teaching.

The sub-title of this volume refers to it as a *primer,* that is, an elementary or introductory textbook. My hope is that it will prove useful as a text in undergraduate theology courses and in lay ministry, diaconate and seminary formation programs. It is my modest hope that it will also find a place in adult education programs. For students desiring a more in-depth treatment of the various topics, much of what is presented in Parts Two and Three of this volume is discussed in more detail and with considerably more documentation, in my earlier work, *Teaching with Authority: A Theology of the Magisterium in the Church.* Each chapter also offers a sample of English language works for further reading. Some are fairly basic while others would doubtless challenge those without an advanced theological education. An introductory text such as this will always depend on the theological scholarship of others. As will be evident in the pages that follow, I have made considerable use of the work of fellow theologians. My goal in this volume was not to provide an original and constructive theology of authority as much as to synthesize and present in an accessible manner the important foundational work on revelation and church teaching authority that has been accomplished in the decades since Vatican II.

The main body of each chapter offers a straightforward theological perspective well within the parameters of Catholic belief. At the end of each chapter I include a section dedicated to "disputed questions." The tradition of attending to *quaestiones disputatae* is an ancient one in Catholic theology. It emerged in the medieval university with the recognition that the careful reading (*lectio*) of an authoritative text often gave rise to lively disagreement regarding a text's adequate interpretation. Thus the *lectio* gave way to the *disputatio* so that a

diversity of interpretations could be given a fair hearing in the
studium. The great historian and expert on the thought of Thomas
Aquinas, M.-D. Chenu, describes well the distinctive character of the
disputation in medieval education:

> From this starting point, the pro and con are brought into play, not
> with the intention of finding an immediate answer, but in order that
> under the action of *dubitatio* [doubt], research be pushed to its limit. A
> satisfactory explanation will be given only on the condition that one
> continue the search to the discovery of what caused the doubt.[1]

This kind of lively discussion is essential for the vitality of the theological enterprise. Although they cannot be treated in any depth in a
book such as this, readers should have some sense of the debates that
are being engaged in academic and ecclesiastical circles. Some of the
positions summarized in this section concern legitimate disagreements
over issues viewed as open questions within mainstream Catholicism.
Other views represent more marginal perspectives. It is my hope that
a précis of contemporary questions and disputes might acquaint the
reader with some of the challenges being addressed in theology and ministry today. Readers wishing to explore some of the disputed questions
will make a good start of it by consulting each chapter's reading list.

I wish to thank those who gave generously of their time to read
and remark upon preliminary drafts of all or part of this volume: James
Bacik, Dennis Doyle, Mary Hines, Thomas O'Meara, Barbara Reid,
Ormond Rush, and John Strynkowski. I am grateful to Elizabeth
Drake for her careful reading of the text and her assistance with the
index. I must also single out the remarkable support and investment of
time and energy that Peter Dwyer, director of the Liturgical Press, has
put into this project. Finally I want to offer my most profound gratitude to the five people who help sustain me daily in my vocation: my
wife Diana, and our four sons, Gregory, Brian, Andrew and David.

INTRODUCTION

Vatican II's
Theology of Revelation

I teach in a state university. A colleague of mine in the philosophy department recently complained that some of the students in her classes were uncritically quoting the Bible in papers they were submitting to her. After trying to voice her irritation tactfully, she finally blurted out in exasperation: "The problem with you Christians is that it always comes down to faith, and then critical thinking goes out the window!" I reassured her that the Christian tradition in general, and my own Roman Catholic tradition in particular, could not be reduced to blind faith and that there was considerable reflection within Christianity on the necessary role of human reason. Nevertheless, her comment does raise an important question for Christianity because there is a sense, of course, in which she is right. Christianity is ultimately premised on the gift of faith. But faith does not come out of nowhere. For Christians, faith is a graced response to something that comes prior to faith. Faith is a response to God's initiative. Christians believe that faith is possible only because God has first come to us in love and has "revealed" God's self to us. We are not left searching the world for an absent God; God comes to us in the wonder of creation, in the sublime beauty of art, in the initial stirrings of the human soul for the "beyond in our midst." The Judeo-Christian tradition claims to have been addressed by God in the history of Israel. Finally, Christians believe, God has spoken an unsurpassable "word" of love in the person of Jesus of Nazareth. This revelation of divine love carries its own authority, the authority of God

1

who is the "Author" of life. This book will attend to the various ways in which the authority of the revealing God is made present and effective in the life of the Church.

Let us begin with two snapshots. The first is of early Christianity around 100 C.E. Christianity was less than seventy years old and was in the process of shifting from a religious movement to a more structured community of believers. Christians believed that, in the person of Jesus Christ, they had encountered the very revelation of God. They did not, however, think of revelation as a distinct body of supernatural knowledge separate from "natural knowledge." Revelation was understood in terms of the person of Jesus of Nazareth as the bearer of God's saving offer. The Good News of Jesus Christ was fearlessly proclaimed by believers. A fluid collection of written texts composed by such important figures as Paul of Tarsus, or originating in churches renowned for their apostolic origins, would soon take on a privileged status in Christianity. Many of these texts, along with texts from the Hebrew Scriptures, would be read before the community when Christians gathered for weekly worship. In some churches, individual leaders were beginning to emerge who were acknowledged to have a special responsibility for the authentic proclamation of the Christian message. However, by the year 100 there was as yet no Bible as we know it today, no developed creeds, no catechisms, no universally recognized episcopal structures.

The second snapshot comes 1850 years later. The year 1950 offered a very different view of how Christians encountered God's revelation. Christianity had long since come to accept the uniquely authoritative role of the Bible. How it was to be interpreted and who had ultimate responsibility for that interpretation had, more than four centuries earlier, become a matter of dispute. Within Catholicism the authority of the Bible was now accompanied by the authority of church traditions, though the relationship between the two was also in dispute. A stable church office with special responsibility for teaching the faith, the episcopate, was now commonly accepted by Catholics and, in varying degrees, by other Christian traditions as well. Divine revelation was still believed to be rooted in Christ, but there was a much greater emphasis on the way in which this revelation could be expressed in objective statements known as dogma and doctrine. Revelation was commonly thought to be a body of supernatural knowledge quite distinct from "natural" knowledge.

At the practical level, a sense of the then dominant notion of revelation was reflected in the process by which an adult was invited into
the Catholic Church. In 1950 it was common for someone desiring
admission into the Roman Catholic Church to receive "instructions"
from the parish priest. In these instructions divine revelation was often
presented as a collection of discrete truths or doctrines. The assumption was that assent to these truths was equivalent to assent to the
Catholic faith. If the inquirer could assent to these teachings, he or she
could be admitted into the Church. Revelation equaled doctrine. Many
scholars refer to this as a *propositional* view of divine revelation. Revelation was seen according to the analogy of verbal communication in
which God literally "spoke" to the biblical prophets and apostles. The
Bible was a record of this verbal communication. In like manner church
teaching was often viewed according to the model of human speech.
Dogmatic propositions were treated like "divine utterances." Revelation, often referred to as the "deposit of the faith," was conceived as a
kind of "filing cabinet" filled with individual files (church doctrines).
To learn "the faith" meant mastering all of the files.

The strength of this approach was its confidence that God was not
some abstract super-Being; the God of the Christian faith could be
known and the Bible and church teaching provided a concrete way to
encounter that God. It affirmed that revelation was not just a vague
feeling or experience, but an objective reality that could be appre-
hended by the human intellect. The danger was that such a stress on
revelation as a collection of objective truths, if taken to extremes, could
lead to various forms of fundamentalism, biblical or ecclesiastical.

VATICAN II'S THEOLOGY OF REVELATION: A TRINITARIAN FRAMEWORK

Vatican II's treatment of divine revelation is a good example of the
council's determination to "return to the sources." The Dogmatic
Constitution on Divine Revelation, *Dei Verbum,* offered a biblically
informed presentation of divine revelation as nothing less than God's
self-gift to humankind in love. It is in this sense that we might properly speak, not of divine words about God, but of a divine "Word"—
the perfect self-expression of God. God's Word, God's personal
self-disclosure, comes to humankind in history in the form of an address. As such, it is an "eventing" of God.

The origins of this dynamic theology of revelation can be found in the Old Testament's use of the Hebrew notion of *dābar* ("word"). We find testimony to the dynamism and effectiveness of God's "word" in the Book of Isaiah:

> For just as from the heavens
> the rain and snow come down
> and do not return there
> till they have watered the earth,
> making it fertile and fruitful,
> Giving seed to him who sows
> and bread to him who eats,
> So shall my word be
> that goes forth from my mouth:
> It shall not return to me void,
> but shall do my will
> achieving the end for which I sent it.

(Isa 55:10-11)

For the biblical author, to speak of God's word was to speak of God's effective action in history. According to the New Testament, "in the fullness of time" God's self-communication becomes not just *a* word from God, but the definitive Word of God, Jesus the Christ. At the beginning of the Gospel of John we find this poetic prologue:

> In the beginning was the Word,
> the Word was with God and the Word was God.
> He was in the beginning with God.
> All things came to be through him,
> and without him nothing came to be.
> What came to be through him was life,
> and this life was the light of the human race . . .
> And the Word became flesh
> and made his dwelling among us,
> and we saw his glory as of the Father's only Son,
> full of grace and truth.   (John 1:1-4, 14)

This passage expresses the conviction that the same word of God, active in creation and present in the Law and prophets, has entered definitively and completely into the world as one of us. Henceforward, in the New Testament, the expression "Word of God" will mean God's creative and saving Word incarnate in Jesus of Nazareth.

In Jesus of Nazareth divine revelation takes the form not of information, facts or even doctrines—revelation comes to the world as a

person. The communication of God's Word to humankind in Jesus is
God's definitive gift of self to the world. According to Christian belief, in Jesus, the Word incarnate, we are given a share in the very life
of God. This is reflected in the opening of the First Letter of John:

> What was from the beginning,
> what we have heard,
> what we have seen with our eyes,
> what we have looked upon
> and touched with our hands
> concerns the Word of life—
> for the life was made visible;
> we have seen it and testify to it
> and proclaim to you the eternal life
> that was with the Father and was made
> visible to us—
> what we have seen and heard
> we proclaim now to you,
> so that you too may have fellowship with us:
> for our fellowship is with the Father
> and with his Son, Jesus Christ.
> We are writing this so that our joy may be complete.
>
> (1 John 1:1-4)

This passage conveys to us the remarkable truth that in Christ, God's
Word Incarnate, we are able to have fellowship with God; the Word
introduces us into relationship with God. This theology of revelation
informed the teaching of the bishops at Vatican II.

The Second Vatican Council affirmed the confidence that Christians ought to possess in the possibility of knowing God, in Christ, by
the power of the Holy Spirit. It insisted on the primacy of Scripture
and the necessity of church doctrine in the life of the Church. At the
same time the council recognized that for many, revelation had been
reduced to a body of information *about* God rather than a living encounter *with* God. Consequently, in *Dei Verbum*, the council affirmed
that revelation was not just a set of statements to be comprehended,
memorized and spouted back to others. "By this revelation, then, the
invisible God from the fullness of his love, addresses men and women
as his friends and lives among them, in order to invite and receive them
into his own company" (DV #2). Divine revelation is presented as a
divine invitation into relationship. This is why, the council says, revelation is summed up in the person of Jesus Christ.

The eternal Word which God shares with us is, in turn, received within our hearts by the power of the Holy Spirit. The council wrote that it is the Holy Spirit "who moves the heart and converts it to God, and opens the eyes of the mind and makes it easy for all to accept and believe the truth" (DV #5). The Spirit leads us into an ever deeper understanding of that revelation. This trinitarian view of revelation— God speaking an eternal Word of Love into our hearts by the power of the Holy Spirit—brings into sharp relief the limits of the propositional view the council was rejecting. Revelation is far more than a set of statements; it is an encounter with the triune God.

In article 3 the council also affirmed that God's plan of salvation, was made manifest "by deeds and words having an inner unity." No longer would it suffice to equate revelation only with words, whether the words of Scripture or of doctrine; revelation also includes God's concrete saving *action* in history, culminating in the death and resurrection of Christ. Although many Christians popularly refer to the Bible as the Word of God, it is more accurate to speak of Scripture as the inspired, *testimony* to the living Word of God. The Bible is not to be equated with revelation; it is a privileged witness to what God has revealed to us. The same Word of God revealed in the Scriptures would continue to abide in the life of the Church, its liturgy, its theological reflection, its doctrinal pronouncements and the daily insight of ordinary believers. The Bible, the liturgy, creeds, doctrinal pronouncements and personal testimony—each in their unique fashion represents diverse expressions or mediations of the one revelation of God in Christ through the power of the Holy Spirit.

Finally, the council taught that God's Word was addressed to the whole people of God. Firmly rejected is the view that God communicates divine revelation primarily to the clergy who then transmit that revelation to the rest of the Church. Rather, the Word of God emerges within the whole Church through a complex set of ecclesial relationships in which all the baptized, professional theologians and the college of bishops, play vital and necessary roles. This was proposed in a number of ways. First, in its treatment of tradition the council affirmed the role not only of the bishops but all the baptized in the processes by which tradition grows and develops. Second, the council acknowledged that the magisterium, as with the entire believing community, is not superior to but rather the servant of the Word of God (DV #10).

REVELATION COMES TO US THROUGH THE MEDIATION OF SYMBOLS: A NEW PHILOSOPHICAL AND THEOLOGICAL FRAMEWORK

The council's theology of revelation anticipates a number of contemporary approaches to revelation. These approaches draw on a philosophy of symbol and suggest that we should view revelation as symbolically mediated.[1] Theologically, the council acknowledged that revelation, in its primary mode, is not the transmission of information, as with the propositional model, but the sharing of divine life. In revelation, God "addresses us as friends" and invites us into relationship.

This revelation is not just a subjective experience; revelation does possess some genuine objective content, as the propositional approach rightly affirms. But here lies the difficulty. God is infinite, incomprehensible mystery, and we are finite creatures. Consequently, God's communication of God's self to us cannot be like my communicating a bus schedule to a friend. Surely as limited creatures we cannot receive God as God is. God cannot be known and mastered the way a beginning chemistry student might strive to master the periodic tables. If God really wishes to communicate with us, God must communicate God's self to us in a manner appropriate to our status as finite, embodied creatures. This is reflected in a medieval dictum, "that which is received is received according to the mode of the receiver" (*quidquid recipitur, recipitur ad modum recipientis*). God comes to us in a manner appropriate to our nature as finite, embodied creatures. And as embodied creatures, the primary way in which we come to know our world is through symbols. We learn through language, concepts, images and metaphors.

Symbols are more than mere signs. Signs point to other realities or bits of discrete information (a red light indicates that we should stop), whereas symbols communicate what the philosopher Paul Ricoeur called a "surplus of meaning." We look at an American flag or a cross—both symbols—and realize that these symbols communicate many different meanings. Indeed, to some extent their meaning changes depending on the context in which the symbol is encountered. An American flag respectfully displayed by a color guard at the beginning of a civic ceremony offers a somewhat different constellation of meanings than an American flag being burned by anti-war protesters. A cross burning on an African-American's front lawn, unfortunately, suggests something quite different from a cross leading a liturgical procession into a church at the beginning of a liturgy.

Revelatory symbols also communicate a surplus of meaning. Sometimes these revelatory symbols are linguistic, as with historical narratives, parables, hymns and doctrinal statements. Sometimes they take the form of distinctive Christian practices, as with the liturgical life of the Church. One might also regard art and architecture as revelatory symbols. The Christian community returns time and again to these symbols because it realizes that these symbols continue to have the power to draw us into relationship *with* God even as they offer us new insight, new meanings *about* God.

Another way of understanding this approach to revelation is to recall the idea of a sacrament. Revelation might be considered sacramental in the sense that, in revelation, as in the sacraments, one encounters God through the medium of some concrete symbol. So the Christian enters into sacramental communion with Christ through the eucharistic symbols of bread and wine. The symbols do not just point to Christ; they make Christ present in the sacrament. Yet we acknowledge that this sacramental presence is not the same as a physical presence; we do not encounter Christ in the Eucharist in the same way in which his disciples encountered him along the shores of Galilee before his death and resurrection. In the Eucharist, Christ is encountered in a manner that we speak of as "real" and sacramental but not physical. Nor is the encounter with God made possible in the sacrament an encounter with an object that can be captured and controlled; rather, God meets us in the sacrament as divine Subject who invites us into loving relationship. To take another example, in the sacrament of marriage, I believe that I truly encounter the love of God in my spouse. And yet I recognize that my wife's love for me, while an authentic sacramental mediation of God's love, does not exhaust God's love. God's love is always more and greater than any created mediation of it.

Catholics acknowledge sacramental presence as a unique mode of encountering God. The idea of sacrament affirms that God communicates to us through the mediation of symbols without being reduced to those symbolic expressions as if there were not always "more" of God to be encountered. Now admittedly, we generally speak of sacraments as mediating God's *grace*, not God's *revelation*. The distinction between grace and revelation is subtle, for both issue from God's desire to share the divine life with us. Perhaps we could say that whereas grace names God offering God's self to us in the realm of human action, revelation names God's self-communication addressing itself specifically to our consciousness.

Understanding revelation as symbolically mediated also has the advantage of highlighting, more than the propositional approach, the role of human experience in the revelatory process.[2] The term "experience" is an ambiguous one. In our culture today "experience" is often used in a purely subjective way, as when we want to emphasize the uniqueness of "my experience." This subjective aspect of human experience is indeed important as it brings to the fore the role of our own personality in shaping how we encounter our world. But experience includes more than this subjective dimension; experience also refers to my engagement with reality. I am always experiencing *something*, and this "something" names the objective aspect of human experience. Experience does not mean being lost in one's own interiority, it means encountering reality in some determinate way.

Another important element in an analysis of human experience is the recognition that human experience is always interpreted. There is really no such thing as a "raw" experience. When we encounter reality, there is a basic dynamism within us that seeks to make sense out of what we have encountered. We try to find *meaning* in our experience. This is never as solitary as we might think. The meanings that we give to our experiences come, at least in part, from the received wisdom of the larger world in which we live—our family, church and culture. At the same time we are free to revise these received meanings, to find new insight in what we experience. Finally, we should note that human experience is always partial. As finite creatures, we never encounter reality in its totality. We encounter our world under some aspect or from some particular perspective. Consequently, human experience is never complete; we change and grow in our grasp of reality.

This very cursory consideration of human experience offers much to our understanding of divine revelation. Revelation is God's self-communication, not in some abstract sense, as if revelation were uttered blindly into the cosmos. God communicates *to us*. As humans we receive that revelation through the prism of human experience in history. Our encounter with the self-revelation of God always has an element of us in the encounter. As we receive that revelation we are bound to interpret it, not privately but from within a number of overlapping interpretive frameworks. Moreover, while from God's side there is nothing lacking in what God communicates to us, from our side, our experience of revelation will always be from a particular perspective and therefore, in some sense, partial or incomplete. This incompleteness must be understood properly. I do not mean that we are missing some vital part of revelation. I am reminded of the Mel Brooks comedy *The History of the World: Part One.* In it there is this wonderful scene in which Brooks plays Moses coming down from Mt. Sinai announcing to the Israelites that he has God's law inscribed on these *three* tablets. Then he stumbles and drops one of them. As it shatters into fragments he pauses, looks up and says, ". . . make that *two* tablets!" To say that revelation is incomplete is not like that. I do not mean that we are missing a tablet, but merely that as finite creatures we encounter the revelation of God from our limited human perspective; there is always "more" to be encountered in God's definitive self-revelation in Christ.

The treatment of revelation throughout this book will presuppose: (1) the council's trinitarian and personalist theology of revelation, (2) the application of the theory of symbolic mediation to our understanding of revelation, and (3) the importance of attending to the ways in which revelation is received and passed on authoritatively through the matrix of human experience. As we address a number of important topics, our theological context will remain committed to this view of revelation as God's eternal offer of self, rendered definitive in Jesus and made present to the believing community through the power of the Spirit. We might speak of this as the trinitarian grammar of divine revelation. At the same time, we will be mindful of the way in which revelation must be understood as encountered through the medium of the symbolic and within the context of human experience. This theological and philosophical framework will be vital for an adequate understanding of the topics to be considered in the chapters that follow.

DISPUTED QUESTIONS

1) With regard to Vatican II's theology of revelation, one of the most contentious issues concerns the nature and scope of divine revelation. According to the Second Vatican Council, "Christ is the mediator and sum total of revelation." Some conciliar texts affirm that God can be encountered outside the

Judeo-Christian tradition. This raises several important questions. The first concerns how revelation is encountered by non-Christians. The council certainly affirms the positive value of such religious traditions. It asserts that they are included in God's "plan of salvation" and that they contain "goodness and truth" (LG #16, see also NA #2). But the council does not directly address itself to the question of whether revelation, properly speaking, is mediated through these traditions. This has been the subject of much debate in the decades since the council.

One school of theologians would read the council texts restrictively, holding that revelation, properly speaking, can be encountered only within the Judeo-Christian tradition. To affirm otherwise, they believe, undercuts the Christian commitment to the uniqueness of Christ. God's offer of salvation to non-Christians manifests itself in ways that can be known only to God. Other theologians contend that the council's recognition of the possibility of salvation for non-Christians presupposes a broader view of revelation. If the non-Christian can be saved, as the council affirmed, doesn't that presuppose that the non-Christian possesses at least some implicit faith? And if they possess an implicit faith, must not that faith be a response to some prior revelation? These theologians wonder, for example, why the Qur'an might not be viewed as a limited mediation of divine revelation. Still other scholars go further and criticize a residual Christian triumphalism in the contention that all revelation finds its term in Christ.

FOR FURTHER READING

Dulles, Avery. *Models of Revelation*. Garden City: Doubleday, 1983.
_____. *Revelation Theology*. New York: Seabury, 1969.
Dupuis, Jacques. *Toward a Christian Theology of Religious Pluralism*. Maryknoll, N.Y.: Orbis, 1997.
Fries, Heinrich. *Fundamental Theology*. Washington, D.C.: Catholic University of America Press, 1996.
Haight, Roger. *Dynamics of Theology*. New York: Paulist, 1990.
Knitter, Paul. *Introducing Theologies of Religions*. Maryknoll, N.Y.: Orbis, 2002.

Lane, Dermot A. *The Experience of God: An Invitation to Do Theology.*
    New York: Paulist, 1981.

O'Collins, Gerald. *Fundamental Theology.* New York: Paulist, 1981.

O'Meara, Thomas F. "Towards a Subjective Theology of Revelation,"
    Theological Studies 36 (1975) 401–27.

PART ONE

THE AUTHORITY OF
SCRIPTURE AND TRADITION

ONE

WHAT DOES IT MEAN TO SAY
THE BIBLE IS INSPIRED?

Often our most basic beliefs and convictions are the ones we find most difficult to define. Virtually every Christian of every denomination would agree that the Bible is inspired. But, press them on what precisely this means, and you will see my point. The range of different views on biblical inspiration is quite wide.

The belief in the inspiration of Scripture is as old as the Church. It was borrowed from ancient Jewish convictions regarding the inspiration of the *Tanak* (the Torah, the Prophets and the Writings) and some sense of biblical inspiration of the *Tanak* is clearly assumed in several New Testament texts:

> All scripture is inspired by God and is useful for teaching, for refutation, for correction, and for training in righteousness, so that one who belongs to God may be competent, equipped for every good work (2 Tim 3:16-17).

> Moreover, we possess the prophetic message that is altogether reliable. You will do well to be attentive to it, as to a lamp shining in a dark place, until day dawns and the morning star rises in your hearts. Know this first of all, that there is no prophecy of scripture that is a matter of personal interpretation, for no prophecy ever came through human will; but rather human beings moved by the holy Spirit spoke under the influence of God (2 Pet 1:19-21).

These consistent declarations of the inspiration of the Scriptures offer little explanation of what they mean by inspiration. Note also that these New Testament texts have in mind the Old Testament when they refer to the Scriptures. The biblical authors were more interested in offering testimony to God's saving work than in offering any particular warrants for the nature of their own authority.

Later generations of Christians were convinced that the Christian texts that were eventually included in the canon of the Bible were also written under divine influence. Yet this did not prevent them from acknowledging the limits of the human authors as well. Early church writers often spoke of God's *accommodation* to the limits of the biblical writers. Nevertheless, theories regarding the nature and extent of divine influence in biblical authorship were few. It was not until the sixteenth century and the Protestant Reformation that theologians, Catholic and Protestant, began devoting attention to the nature and limits of the Christian claims to the authority of the Bible.

THEORIES OF BIBLICAL INSPIRATION

The word "inspiration" derives from a Latin root which means to "breathe into." Inspiration, then, is the word Christians have given to name their conviction that the Bible is "God-breathed," that the texts themselves, or at least their religious content, come by way of some special form of the Spirit's influence. Robert Gnuse, in his helpful book *The Authority of the Bible*, offers several different theories of biblical inspiration. The account of inspiration that follows is indebted to his work, although I have adjusted his categories slightly, reducing them to two basic views: verbal inspiration, and non-verbal inspiration.[1] Each of these views, in turn, contains within them several variants.

Verbal Inspiration

One general approach to biblical inspiration focuses on the biblical text itself and the ways in which divine influence can be asserted in the production of the biblical text. There are two basic versions of this approach: strict verbal inspiration and limited verbal inspiration.

Strict Verbal Inspiration

For many Christians, to say that the Bible is the Word of God means, in fact, that the Bible consists of the "words of God." That is, they believe that the particular words of the Bible, in the original languages in which they were written, were given to the biblical authors in a process that can only be described as a kind of spiritual dictation. The closest analog for this in other traditions is Islam, which holds that the words of the Qur'an were dictated to the prophet Mohammed through the angel Gabriel. For Islam, only the Arabic text of the Qur'an is considered the inspired text. Few Christians go this far. They readily grant the need for vernacular translations, but many do treat the Bible as whole and entire, the words of God.

This approach to inspiration assumes that there was an identifiable group of biblical authors who could be distinguished from the larger community of Israel and early Christianity and who were subject to a distinct form of divine influence in their authorship. Proponents of this view admit that the biblical authors wrote in their own style and in keeping with their own education, but they insist that the authors' intellects were directed by God to communicate divine truth wholly and infallibly.

This understanding of inspiration is relatively recent in the history of Christianity. It emerged only over the last two centuries. Though one can find Catholic proponents, the theory found its fullest development in the nineteenth-century world of Protestantism, largely in reaction to the rise of historical-critical scholarship (that approach to biblical scholarship that studies the Bible according to the methods historians employ in the study of any historical text) in some liberal Protestant circles. Interestingly, it may well have been the Catholic emphasis on a theology of papal infallibility that led Protestant scholars to develop a parallel theory of biblical infallibility.

Strict verbal inspiration presupposes the propositional model of revelation discussed in the introduction. It entails a commitment to the complete and total inerrancy of the Bible in all matters. The Bible is held to be without error in every aspect: history, science and culture as well as in regard to religious truth.

One question immediately raised by this approach concerns the problem of the biblical text itself. We do not have any original manuscript of a book of the Bible. Prior to the discovery of the Dead Sea scrolls, our oldest manuscripts for the Old Testament were dated to the ninth century. Even now the oldest manuscripts of the whole New Testament (the Codex Vaticanus and Codex Sinaiticus) date back only to the fourth century (though we have some small fragments dating all the way to the early second century). Not surprisingly, given the extended period of time between the original authorship of a biblical text and the date of the manuscript copies we possess, these manuscripts do not agree with one another in every detail; individual manuscripts often offer variant readings of a given passage. Proponents of strict verbal inspiration are aware of these difficulties and usually respond that biblical inspiration only concerns the original text and not the copies. They are willing to recognize the fallibility of manuscript copies, while insisting that the minor discrepancies that might emerge through scribal errors do not in any way affect the revealed content of the Bible.

Though this view of biblical inspiration and inerrancy is quite popular in Christian circles, many Christians find difficulties with this approach. It focuses on the divine origins of biblical texts without attending sufficiently to the humanity of the authors who actually composed them. Just as early heretical groups denied the humanity of Christ because they could not see how Christ could be both human and divine at the same time, so some Christians today do not see how the Bible can be both human and divine at the same time.

The popular consequence of this approach to inspiration and inerrancy is the use of the Bible as a kind of "owner's manual" intended to provide authoritative answers on matters as diverse as the origins of human life, investment strategies and the choice of a spouse. Moreover, one must consider the possibility that strict verbal inspiration, by focusing on the absolute inerrancy of the Bible, focuses more on defense of the text itself than on the message the biblical texts are supposed to communicate.

Limited Verbal Inspiration

An alternative account that still emphasizes the inspiration of biblical texts themselves might be called limited verbal inspiration. In many ways, this is a modern version of the early church notion of divine accommodation in which it was thought that, while God inspired the biblical authors, it was necessary for God to make "accommodations" to the limited knowledge of those authors. Some medieval thinkers adopted a similar approach, distinguishing between God's role as the primary cause in the authorship of biblical texts, and the human authors as the secondary or instrumental causes of the same texts. This theory allowed these medieval thinkers to affirm that God communicated divine revelation through, rather than in spite of, the created freedom and limitations of the biblical authors.

Current proponents of this view often draw on contemporary developments in biblical studies. For example, it is now commonly acknowledged by biblical scholars, Catholic and Protestant, that the adequate interpretation of a biblical text requires that the interpreter attend to: (1) the intention of the author as best as it can be discerned; (2) the historical and social context in which a text was written; (3) the particular literary genre or form that was employed in the text; (4) the history of a particular text which might have developed from an early oral stage and gone through various revisions on the way to the final form encountered in the Bible; (5) the various symbolic and mythological uses of narrative; (6) the interpretation of a particular text within the context of the whole of biblical testimony; (7) the way the text has been read within the tradition of the Church.

Adherents of this view will acknowledge a unique divine influence on the biblical authors but contend that this influence would not have precluded the biblical authors communicating divine revelation from within an historically and culturally conditioned framework. They remain committed to the inerrancy of the Bible, with the significant qualification that the Bible is without error only as regards divine revelation, but not as regards historical or scientific matters.

There are obvious advantages to such a model as it allows a person to overcome the many instances where biblical testimony on matters of science and history appear irreconcilable with our modern understanding of such matters. This view also fits well with Vatican II's shift away from a propositional view of revelation to one that focuses more on biblical testimony to the one divine self-communication offered in Christ through the power of the Holy Spirit. On the other hand, some critics have also warned that, in practice, it may be difficult to distinguish between biblical content concerned with divine revelation and that pertaining strictly to questions of science and history.

Non-Verbal or Content Inspiration

What both of the above approaches share is a concern with the role of divine influence in the production of the biblical texts themselves. Problems with manuscript discrepancies and our knowledge of the long, multi-stage, historical process that produced many texts have led some scholars to reject this focus on the written texts.

Inspiration of Ideas and Persons

One way to do this is to distinguish between the human words that form the biblical text, and the underlying ideas or religious content. This theory holds that God does not actually form the words in the mind of the author but rather inspires an idea or insight which the author communicates in their own words. One can go back to the third century and find Christian thinkers who viewed inspiration more in terms of the divine influence in the production of ideas than on the inspiration of texts. The great Alexandrian theologian Origen understood inspiration as a kind of "illumination" of the biblical author that gave a relatively greater place for human agency. Consequently, he was able to allow for the possibility of error in biblical texts. In the nineteenth century, some scholars, like John Henry Newman, held that the Bible was only inspired as regarded faith and morals. In the same century, influential Catholic theologians, like Giovanne Perrone and Johann Baptist Franzelin, affirmed that the biblical authors received ideas by way of divine assistance but that the words chosen by the authors were of completely human origin.

Another variant of this approach focused, not on the idea "behind" the text, but rather on some religious experience that affected the author. Inspiration, in this view, is really not related to the biblical text at all, but only to some religious experience which would influence or shape the author's writing. Here one might link the inspiration of St. Paul to his own conversion experience on the road to Damascus, for example. To say that the Bible is inspired in this sense is simply to say that the Bible gives testimony to the religious experiences of its authors. The principal danger of this approach is the possible reduction of the Bible to a collection of subjective accounts of religio-mystical encounters with very little objective content. It also makes it very difficult to distinguish between an "idea" and the verbal expression of that "idea." However, this approach has the obvious advantage of avoiding the problems of inerrancy that accompany a claim that the biblical text itself is inspired.

Social Inspiration

Up to this point, all of the theories of inspiration that we have considered have focused on the Holy Spirit's influence on a particular biblical author. As such all of these theories could be considered "psychological" theories of inspiration. However, these psychological theories face a fundamental challenge in the face of modern biblical scholarship: if many biblical texts emerged out of a multi-stage process of development, sometimes being preserved through generations of oral transmission before being transcribed as a written text, then how does one identify the author who is the subject of divine inspiration? The solution for the Protestant biblical scholar Paul Achtemeier, the Catholic biblical scholar John McKenzie, and the Catholic systematic theologian Karl Rahner, was to resituate inspiration within the life of the early Christian community. Inspiration is presented as a charism active within all the complex human interactions of the early Christian community that ultimately gave rise to the biblical texts.

In our world today, concerns about plagiarism and copyright violations reflect the importance we give to the authorship of a literary work. This was not the case in the ancient world. Many biblical texts were written anonymously, with biblical authorship ascribed to them only generations after they were written. Given this reality, it only makes sense, proponents of this theory contend, to focus on the Spirit's movement within the whole community.

This theory accords well with a significant but generally overlooked feature of the very origins of Christianity. Jesus of Nazareth did not bequeath to his followers a written text of any kind. He wrote no memoirs, no autobiography, no written rules of conduct. Rather than leave a written text, Jesus called forth a community of disciples. Jesus' own actions suggest that he put higher stock in community formation than the production of a written text.

VATICAN II'S TREATMENT OF THE TOPIC

In the nineteenth century Catholic scholars like Newman and Franzelin grappled with ways to affirm the Bible's inspiration while allowing some room for non-revelatory error. However, Pope Leo XIII's encyclical *Providentissimus Deus* (1893) appeared to put an end to such theories with his assertion that the Bible was without error in all matters, sacred and profane. The climate for reconsidering the question of inspiration and inerrancy did improve considerably when Pope Pius XII published his encyclical *Divino Afflante Spiritu* in 1943, permitting Catholic biblical scholars to make full use of the tools of modern biblical scholarship. When the Second Vatican Council opened nineteen years later, the Catholic Church was only beginning to experience the first fruits of this development. Consequently, the council members were inclined to proceed quite cautiously on questions related to the authority of the Bible.

Biblical Inspiration

The preparatory draft on divine revelation that was sent to the bishops on the eve of the council offered an account of divine revelation that came very close to the model of strict verbal inspiration discussed above. In contrast, the final version, what became *Dei Verbum,* offers a much more modest theory of biblical inspiration, acknowledging the role of human agency in the authorship of Scripture. This shift is often very subtle. Article 11 affirms that Scripture was written under the inspiration of the Holy Spirit while carefully refraining from support of any one theory. The council refers to God as the "author" of Scripture, but it refrains from identifying God as the *principal* author as did an earlier version. In response to views of inspiration that treated the human authors as automatons, this same article also states that the human authors made full use of their own powers and abilities such that they also may be called "true authors" of the Bible. Where an earlier version of article 7 referred to the "dictation of the holy Spirit," the final text refers to a "prompting of the holy Spirit," a much more modest description of God's action and one that left more room for human freedom. The council members seemed well aware that there was much more constructive theological work to be done regarding a theology of inspiration. They were content to make several general assertions while leaving the door open for further theological development.

Biblical Inerrancy

The council did feel it necessary to address the question of biblical inerrancy. A proper appreciation for the subtlety of the bishops' approach requires that we look at the history of the text that dealt with this question. An early version of the schema on divine revelation proposed a doctrine of "total inerrancy," holding that the Scriptures were, in their entirety, completely without error regarding all truths "religious or profane" *(re religiosa et profana).* The reference to "profane truths" *(veritates profanae)* was the subject of much discussion. Many bishops claimed that this suggested an almost monophysitic view of biblical inspiration and inerrancy—in other words, the humanity of the biblical text was in danger of being absorbed into divine authorship. These bishops were well aware of certain historical difficulties found in the Bible. The classic example often cited was Mark 2:26, which recounts David entering the house of God under the high priest Abiathar when, according to 1 Samuel 21:1ff., David did so not under Abiathar but under his father Ahimelech. One might also mention discrepancies in the Gospel regarding at what point in Christ's ministry (at the beginning or the end) the so called "cleansing of the temple" took place, or the disagreement among the gospels regarding whether Christ's last supper occurred on Passover or not.

On October 2, 1964 Cardinal König of Vienna gave a crucial speech in which he warned that the bishops could not afford to ignore the findings of modern biblical exegesis that certain factual data of history and the natural sciences contained in the Bible were "deficient." His address was well received by the assembly. The general sentiment of the bishops was, on the one hand, to avoid any sense that only "parts" of Scripture were inspired, while on the other hand allowing for the place of human limitations and/or deficiencies in the text.

The decision was made to avoid the religious/profane truths distinction altogether. A final formulation was arrived at only through tortuous negotiation in which even the pope weighed in with his views on the matter. The final text reads:

> Since, therefore, all that the inspired authors, or sacred writers, affirm should be regarded as affirmed by the holy Spirit, we must acknowledge that the books of scripture, firmly, faithfully and without error, teach that truth *which God, for the sake of our salvation, wished to see confided to the sacred scriptures* (DV #11).

The key was the formulation, "for the sake of our salvation." This shifted the emphasis from the content of Scripture, that is the biblical text itself, to the divine intention. Rather than risk dividing Scripture into religious and profane truths, the council held that inspiration and inerrancy be viewed from the perspective of God's salvific intention. *All* Scripture was inspired, but inspired with a view to salvation, not with a view to historical or scientific accuracy. The scientific and historical framework of biblical texts is to be read as a medium for the communication of God's offer of salvation.

This more modest view constituted a subtle but important departure from the total inerrancy that follows from a theory of strict verbal inspiration. The council's perspective was carefully crafted to admit the possibility of human limitations, deficiencies and even errors entering into the authorship of the sacred texts, but in such a way that

God's saving truth was still faithfully communicated through the medium of the entire biblical testimony.

CONCLUDING REFLECTIONS

If the council's own approach hovers between limited verbal inspiration and the inspiration of ideas, post-conciliar reflection has been more inclined to move toward revised theories of social inspiration. This is particularly true for Catholic theologians who are more prone to situate the authority of the Bible within the authority of the Church. However, this move toward social theories of inspiration need not preclude appeal to more psychological theories, for as several proponents of social inspiration have observed, a charism given to a community still, in diverse ways, must be exercised through individual human actions.

We should not be surprised to discover some of the difficulties that theologians have had in arriving at an adequate theory of biblical inspiration. The dynamics of human discovery and the workings of the creative process have always had a mysterious and ineffable quality that resists schematization. Artists have always struggled to explain how some creative idea came to them. Theology, however, brings to light further difficulties. The daunting task of developing an adequate theory of biblical inspiration is really but one example of a larger theological quandary that has occupied theologians from the beginning of Christianity—how to explain the mysterious collaboration of divine and human agency. The temptation is to fall prey to a kind of zero-sum theory. The human and the divine are placed in a zero-sum relationship such that the emphasis on one term in the equation requires de-emphasizing the other. An excellent historical example of this can be seen in the so called *De Auxiliis* controversy between Dominicans and Jesuits in the sixteenth century. The Dominicans emphasized divine initiative in the life of grace, often at the expense of human freedom, while the Jesuits were inclined to emphasize human freedom at the expense of divine initiative. Christological controversies betrayed similar tendencies. Over-emphasis on Christ's divine nature inevitably compromised Christ's humanity and vice versa. Difficulties raised by the question of biblical inspiration are similar in nature.

Too often forgotten is the Christian conviction that God is not another created agent competing with physical causal events or the work of human agents. God is the ground and source of all forms of agency. God is the source of life and freedom that makes it possible for a human person to exercise their freedom. Applied to our understanding of divine inspiration, this suggests that the influence of the Holy Spirit on the early biblical community need not be set off against their created, historically and culturally circumscribed freedom. Rather, inspiration can be understood as God's revealing what God wishes "for the sake of our salvation" precisely through the very real limitations and even biases of the biblical authors and/or their communities. This is the enduring mystery of God-With-Us.

The theories of verbal inspiration, and the preoccupation with inerrancy that accompanies them, are the result of a reliance on a propositional model of revelation. When we consider revelation as symbolically mediated, the problems of inerrancy are, to a certain extent, side-stepped. If Scripture is the symbolic mediation of divine revelation, then it faithfully communicates divine revelation through the created, human medium of biblical testimony. An honest admission of the human authorship of biblical texts does not in any way negate the genuine influence of the Spirit nor does it undermine the integrity of what is communicated through the Scriptures, namely God's self gift to humankind in love. God's revelation may be disclosed in the Scriptures, but we appropriate it only through the hard work of critical and communal interpretation. We must set aside any simplistic views of revelation that see it as nothing more than a set of propositions to be proved and defended.

This is what Christians mean when they hold that the Bible must be read in faith. They recognize, of course, that the Bible can be read and comprehended apart from faith. Many colleges and universities offer courses on the Bible as literature, an altogether legitimate undertaking. Christians believe, however, that the same texts read by one person solely as literature can also be read through the lens of faith in such a way that the literary content is not denied, but becomes the medium for encountering divine revelation. The fruit of that encounter is an experience of communion between the reader/hearer and the God who addresses them. To say that Scripture is "inerrant" is to affirm that the Bible gives faithful testimony to God's saving offer and, when read in faith, brings one into saving communion with God.

DISPUTED QUESTIONS

1) Feminist theology has raised a particular set of difficulties for any theology of inspiration. Feminist biblical scholarship has called for the application of a "hermeneutic of suspicion" in the interpretation of biblical texts. By "hermeneutic of suspicion" they mean a critical criterion that requires the biblical interpreter to adopt a stance of deliberate "suspicion" toward the possibility of bias in a given text. This suspicion concerns the extent to which a given biblical text might reflect patriarchal bias (patriarchy refers to a set of cultural, legal, economic and political relationships that assert male superiority and dominance over women). Such a bias is reflected in the assumption, whether implicit or explicit, that maleness is somehow the norm for understanding human experience and, to that extent, also for understanding God. For many feminist scholars, the pervasive presence of such a patriarchal bias in the Bible raises particular difficulties for any claim to biblical inspiration. At the minimum it suggests that the acknowledgement of human deficiencies in biblical texts must go beyond the spheres of science and history to include systemic cultural bias. Feminist scholars also wonder whether patriarchal views of authority in the Church will not influence how Christians understand the authority of the Bible. They contend that, too often, appeals to the authority of the Bible have been used to assert the dominance of church leadership over members of the community and particularly women.

In response to this critique, other scholars have contended that the appropriate Christian hermeneutic for interpreting biblical texts should be governed, not by systemic suspicion, but by trust. Without denying the historically and culturally conditioned nature of the Bible, critics of feminist biblical criticism insist that the inspired character of such texts precludes systemic bias and requires that one accept the essential trustworthiness of biblical texts as faithful testimonies to the Word of God.

2) Some scholars question, in the light of contemporary inter-religious dialogue, whether it is necessary to speak of divine inspiration as unique to and exclusive of Christian biblical texts. If, with Vatican II, we can affirm the truth and goodness to be found within other religious traditions, and if all truth

and goodness find their ultimate source in God, then is it not possible to assert divine influence, in some fashion, in the production of sacred texts within other religious traditions, e.g., the Qur'an for Islam or the Upanishads for Hinduism? Critics would respond that such a view seriously weakens the traditional Christian understanding of biblical inspiration and threatens traditional Christian claims regarding the unique revelation of God in Christ testified to in the Scriptures.

3) Most of the approaches to biblical inspiration have focused on divine influence with respect to individual authors, communities or texts. But some scholars today contend that one must also consider the possibility of inspiration or divine assistance with respect to the contemporary *reader* or *hearer* of a biblical text. They ask whether the process of reading or hearing a text and interpreting it within a contemporary context might also be subject to divine influence.

FOR FURTHER READING

Achtemeier, Paul J. *The Inspiration of Scripture: Problems and Proposals.* Philadelphia: Westminster, 1980.

Barr, James. *Holy Scripture: Canon, Authority, Criticism.* Philadelphia: Westminster, 1983.

_____. *The Scope and Authority of the Bible.* Philadelphia: Westminster, 1980.

Burtchaell, James Tunstead. *Catholic Theories of Biblical Inspiration since 1810: A Review and Critique.* Cambridge: Cambridge University Press, 1969.

Countryman, William. *Biblical Authority or Biblical Tyranny?* Philadelphia: Fortress, 1981.

Fiorenza, Elizabeth Schüssler. *Bread not Stone: The Challenge of Feminist Biblical Interpretation.* Boston: Beacon Press, 1984.

Gnuse, Robert. *The Authority of the Bible: Theories of Inspiration, Revelation and the Canon of Scripture.* New York: Paulist, 1985.

Law, David R. *Inspiration.* New York: Continuum, 2001.

Lienhard, Joseph T. *The Bible, the Church, and Authority: The Canon of the Christian Bible in History and Theology.* Collegeville: The Liturgical Press, 1995.

Pontifical Biblical Commission. *The Interpretation of the Bible in the Church.* Edited by J. L. Houlden. London: SCM Press, 1995.

Russell, Letty, ed. *Feminist Interpretation of the Bible.* Philadelphia: Westminster, 1985.

Schneiders, Sandra M. *The Revelatory Text: Interpreting the New Testament as Sacred Scripture.* New York: HarperCollins, 1991.

Sundberg, Albert. "The Bible Canon and the Christian Doctrine of Inspiration," *Interpretation* (1974) 352–71.

Vawter, Bruce. *Biblical Inspiration. Theological Resources.* Philadelphia: Westminster, 1972.

TWO

WHAT IS THE CANON
OF THE BIBLE?

The word "Bible" conjures a number of images. For some it may call to mind a large family Bible kept in a prominent place in one's home and filled with family genealogical data. Or it may bring to mind one's own personal Bible, with favorite passages marked for easy reference. We might think of a television evangelist, Bible in hand, preaching on the meaning of a particular passage. As I write these words on my laptop in a hotel room, I know there is a copy of the Bible in the drawer to the nightstand, provided by Gideons International. Whatever the particular recollection, it almost certainly will assume a bound volume, mass-produced for individual purchase and use.

When we consider the appropriate uses of the Bible, many would cite the importance of private Bible reading for spiritual edification. Others might mention its use in faith-based Bible studies constituted by small groups of believers. Many will look to the Bible as a source for particular answers to key decisions or as a warrant for a particular belief. Consequently, it may come as a shock to realize that for almost sixteen centuries few Christians owned their own Bible.[1] Indeed, if by Bible we mean a single collection of all the canonical texts, the first true "Bible" was probably St. Jerome's Vulgate produced in the late fourth century. For almost a thousand years, copies of biblical texts were compiled in multi-volume collections. These collections were relatively rare and kept in monasteries, churches, the private libraries of nobles and, later, universities. They were used not for private edification or apologetic disputation but for display, communal worship and formal study by scholars, monks and clerics.

The first truly "portable" Bible existing as a single-bound volume emerged only in the thirteenth century, and only in that century did the order of the books within the Bible and the designation of chapter and verse become standardized. Bibles of a size comparable to the modern pocket Bible were developed in Paris in the late thirteenth century. They were made popular by the newly created mendicant religious orders, the Franciscans and Dominicans, who wanted a Bible that could be carried in their habit as they traveled from town to town, exercising their itinerant preaching ministry. These Bibles were produced in the thousands for the friars' use, and the widespread exposure given to these Bibles by the friars undoubtedly lead other wealthy and educated persons to obtain copies. Nevertheless, Bibles still would not have been the common possession of individual believers.

The true revolution in the popularity and use of Bibles begins with Johann Gutenberg's invention of a moveable-type printing press. In the mid-fifteenth century, Gutenberg began mass-producing a two-volume Latin Bible which he commercially marketed as a "lectern Bible" to be used in churches and monasteries as well as for private readings in the households of devout, educated laypersons. Between 1520 and 1550, the fortuitous synchronicity of Gutenberg's technology, Luther's vernacular biblical translations, and the Reformation commitment to the priority of the Bible as a religious authority, led to what can only be called the "domestication of the Bible in Europe."[2] In consequence, it was only in the sixteenth century that the Bible acquired the authority that many today attach to it, for only in the sixteenth century did the Bible begin to reach thousands of people who had never encountered it outside of community worship.

It is one of the truly singular features of the Protestant Reformation that the Bible became an independent source of religious authority to ordinary Christians. Prior to the Reformation the authority of the Bible was, by necessity, conjoined to the authority of the Church; it was almost exclusively in the context of church life, in the liturgy, in the university and in the monastery, that the authority of the Bible was invoked. After the sixteenth century it would be possible to appeal to the authority of the Bible without having, at the same time, to appeal to the authority of the Church. From that time on the question of how to construe the proper relationship between the authority of the Church and the authority of the Bible would be a source of division within Christianity.

THE ORIGINS OF THE CANON OF THE BIBLE

Seen from another perspective, the Bible is not just a book that we keep on our nightstand. Christians understand the Bible to consist of a defined "canon" of sacred texts. The term "canon" is derived from the Greek word referring to a "reed" or instrument of measure. In its early church usage "canon" referred not to the Bible but to the living rule of faith, the preached good news of Jesus the Christ. This was the first "measure" of the Christian faith. The development of a written canon occurred only very slowly.

The Canon of the Old Testament

The Old Testament itself was composed over a period of almost one thousand years. Much of the literature first appeared in oral form as stories, myths, moral codes, hymns and aphorisms. What they shared was their testimony to the gracious and faithful activity of the Hebrew God in human history. Over time, oral traditions took primitive written form followed by a subsequent process in which these texts were further combined and edited. Particular passages, sometimes placed one after another within a particular book of the Bible, were often written at very different times. Some of the book of Exodus might have been written as early as 1200 B.C.E. only to be combined with other traditions written as late as 500 B.C.E.

The idea of a collection of sacred writings emerged only gradually among the people of Israel. Many scholars note the significance of the seventh-century Deuteronomic reforms associated with the reign of King Josiah. This period of great reform involved re-weaving ancient texts into a new historical framework that offered a master tale of God's dealings with Israel grounded in the giving of the law to Moses. Many of the books of the Old Testament found their final form during this period. The collection of books that resulted went a long way toward shifting the locus of Israelite faith from an oral Torah to a set of sacred writings. An early collection of written texts were likely to have been particularly important for the Israelites as they sought to preserve their identity while in exile. It was during the Babylonian exile and its aftermath that other books would be added to this loose collection.

Judaism preserved from early on, then, a sense of sacred texts that they believed were inspired. But they did not engage in any formal process to separate these texts from others. The emergence of a true "canon," in the sense of a closed and definitive list of texts that were treated as uniquely authoritative, would come later than was once commonly thought. Disagreement regarding when Judaism moved from a collection of sacred texts to a true canon helps explain the presence of two distinctly different lists of the books contained in the Old Testament.

The Problem of Different Canons

Many Christians are aware that there are differences between the Catholic and Protestant canon of the Old Testament. The traditional explanation of this difference was built on the commonly held assumption that in the first century of Christianity Judaism possessed two different lists of its own sacred texts: one was employed by Palestinian Jews (and referred to as the Palestinian canon) and presupposed the tradition that the Jewish canon was closed at the time of Ezra (ca. 4–5th centuries B.C.E.). The second, longer canon was thought to have been adopted by Jews in Northern Africa (often referred to as the Alexandrian canon) which included books written after the time of Ezra during the so called "Second Temple" period. This canon was enshrined in the Greek Septuagint.

The existence of these two distinct canons was commonly assumed in the fourth century when Christians were compiling their own "canon" of sacred texts. The majority of early Christian communities followed St. Augustine and the church of North Africa in adopting a list of books thought to be based on the Alexandrian canon. St. Jerome, representing a minority view at the time, proposed acceptance only of the Palestinian canon. Western Christianity ultimately followed St. Augustine and accepted the larger canon of Jewish texts.

This rough consensus would be maintained until the time of the Protestant Reformation. Luther's own views on the canon emerged only gradually. Early in his writing he seems to have accepted those books included in the larger canon. However, in his debates with Johann Maier of Eck, he was confronted with 2 Maccabees 12:46 that seemed to support the Catholic doctrine of purgatory. This raised questions about the canonicity of these later Jewish texts and led Luther to adopt the position of Jerome in rejecting the canonicity of all books written after the purported closing of the canon by Ezra. Thus the distinction between the Protestant and Catholic canons was traced to the assumption of both Augustine and Jerome that there were two canons, one Palestinian that held for the closing of the canon with Ezra, and a second longer Alexandrian canon. Catholics typically refer to those books included in their canon but not that of the Protestants as "deutero-canonical" books, while Protestants will generally refer to them as "apocrypha."

Contemporary scholarship, however, has challenged several features of this classical explanation of the different canons. For one thing, it now appears that at the time of Jesus there was no fixed Jewish canon of any kind. Judaism certainly believed in a set of inspired writings, but the idea that these writings needed to be definitively set apart from other literature had not yet developed. Indeed, most scholars now reject the idea, accepted by both Jerome and Augustine, that there ever were two distinct Jewish canons. It now appears that it was only well after 70 C.E. that Judaism became concerned with identifying a precise biblical canon. Christianity itself did not focus on the need for a true canon of its own until the late second century. In other words, the early Christian acceptance of the later works like 1 and 2 Maccabees had nothing to do with assumptions about a prior Jewish canon because there was, as yet, no such canon. Some Jews accepted later books as authoritative and others did not. Christian communities seem to have come to their own judgment largely based on more pragmatic considerations, with the criterion of liturgical usage playing a significant role. The influential list offered by the North African Council of Hippo reflects that Church's dependence on the contents of the Septuagint manuscripts available to them at the time.

The Development of the New Testament Canon

As with the texts of the Old Testament, many of those of the New Testament, particularly the Gospels, likely emerged out of a multistage process beginning with oral materials. Most of the New Testament literature was written between about 50 and 110 C.E. Paul's letters soon found wide circulation and later generations would emulate his approach, even to the point of writing under his name, as with the pastoral letters. Later citations from early church writers suggest that the four Gospels and many of Paul's letters were used widely among the churches. As with the Old Testament, for several centuries there were Christian *Scriptures* before there was a Christian *canon*. The eventual need to identify a closed canon developed only gradually. As heretical movements emerged that appeared to threaten the integrity of the Christian faith, two strategies were employed in tandem: (1) the development of a biblical canon that could be used as the measure of authentic Christian faith and (2) the development of a church office empowered to preserve the one apostolic faith. We will concern ourselves with the second development in Part Two of this volume. The development of a true "canon" that became not just a collection of texts but a closed list of texts given uniquely authoritative status took place, for the most part, in the third and fourth centuries.

But how did these communities set about determining which texts were or were not "canonical"? Several criteria came into play. First was the question of *apostolicity,* that is, a text's connection with a known apostle of Christ. In fact, the apostolicity of a text may have been more a matter of legend, but *the claim* to apostolicity remained a significant factor in determining the status of a text. A second criterion concerned the importance of the community from which a text emerged. So, for example, the disruption of early Palestinian Christianity may explain why no strictly Palestinian text ever found its way into the canon, whereas several texts from Syria (Matthew, James and Jude) were accepted. A third criterion was the text's conformity with the "rule of faith." No text could be accepted into the canon that proposed teachings at odds with the received apostolic faith. This helps explain why certain texts with more idiosyncratic theological perspectives (e.g., Hebrews and Revelation) only won acceptance into the canon at a relatively late date and only after considerable debate. Finally, we must acknowledge the importance of liturgical usage. The liturgical use of a text often played a decisive role in its inclusion in the canon.

Within the Orthodox traditions even today, the question of liturgical use has been determinative. The Orthodox see the Bible as the principal "prayer book of the church."[3] For them all questions of canonicity are ultimately questions of those books that the Church shall use in its liturgy. This position is more distinctive than may first appear. As the Eastern Orthodox biblical scholar Michael Prokurat puts it:

> In saying Scripture is liturgical, we do not mean to say merely that liturgy is scriptural; but moreover that what was originally liturgy became Scripture. Scripture had its emergence and continued existence in the liturgy, the liturgical life of the Temple and Church, the communal prayers of the people of God.[4]

Although the Christian canon became fixed, for the most part, by the end of the fourth century, we should be careful not to make too much of this. Within that canon a core set of books existed that were broadly accepted and quite influential in sustaining the faith of the early community. Other books were more controversial and, though technically canonical, never received the same weight within the tradition. Still other texts that were not finally included in the canon would remain quite influential for many Christian communities. Even after the canon became "fixed" in the late fourth century, disagreements would continue, in varying degrees, for centuries. Many distinguished figures over the centuries expressed doubts of one kind or another regarding the contents of the canon, including: Pope Gregory the Great, St. John Damascene, Hugh of St. Victor and Cardinal Cajetan.

Distinguishing Questions of Canonicity from Questions of Inspiration

The determination of a canon was, at least initially, not about separating inspired books from non-inspired books, but a matter of determining which books were reliable witnesses to the ancient faith. What distinguishes the canon from other works, in other words, is not inspiration, but the Church's Spirit-assisted judgment regarding the reliable testimony of these works. As Robert Gnuse put it: "The ancient church did not bestow authority on the various works incorporated into the canon, it merely recognized the authority which already lay therein."[5]

The idea that only the canonical books of the Bible could lay claim to inspiration now appears to have had its origin in later Jewish literature (after the first century) in which some rabbis taught that inspiration could be found only in the sacred writings from Moses to Ezra. The early Christian community eventually came upon this notion and accepted it. However, the more ancient Christian perspective is described succinctly by Sundberg:

> Thus, in forming the canon, the church acknowledged and established the Bible as the measure or standard of inspiration in the church, not as the totality of it. What concurs with canon is of like inspiration; what does not is not of God.[6]

To help explore this distinction between canonicity and inspiration, consider the following thought experiment.

Suppose that archaeologists were to discover a lost letter of St. Paul, his *Second* Letter to the Romans, let's say. After careful study, biblical scholars conclude that it is indeed an authentic letter of Paul. What should the Christian churches do? Should they expand the canon of the Bible to include the book?

An affirmative answer confuses the question of inspiration and canonicity, for while one might legitimately conclude that the text was inspired, this does not make it necessarily canonical. The canon was established in the early Church as a way of designating books whose inspiration was authenticated and therefore *could serve as a norm for the faith of the churches.* A book found only today could not qualify, not because of any questions regarding its "inspired" character, but because it has not served as a norm for the faith of the churches. It has not served as an ecclesial benchmark for the development of our liturgy, theology, spirituality and church discipline.

THE SIGNIFICANCE OF A BIBLICAL CANON FOR AUTHORITY IN THE CHURCH

One of the most important functions of the biblical canon is to remind us that Christianity is an historical religion; it is not grounded in a collection of eternal myths but in a set of historical accounts of God's saving action on behalf of humanity. In other words, Christians do not believe that they can "make it up as they go." Of course, as we shall see in the next chapter, Christianity is also an innovative religion that accepts the possibility of emerging new insight about the faith. The Christian faith is always in some sense tethered to its past, even if that tether can appear quite elastic at times. The canonical books of the Bible anchor that elastic tether. These sacred texts stand as a norm for the Christian faith, a benchmark against which all further expressions of Christian belief and all further Christian activity must be measured. As scholastic theologians would later write in a wonderful exercise in Latin alliteration, Scripture is the *norma normans non normata* (the norm which norms all other expressions of the faith but which is not itself normed).

The authority of the Bible is also situated within the life of the community. Our consideration of the formation of the biblical canon can leave no doubt but that the Bible itself emerged out of the prior life of communities of faith (both of Israel and early Christianity). The Scriptures are the end result of a centuries old process by which human experiences of the saving God were given first oral and then written expression as dynamic traditions, only much later finding their final form in the biblical texts.

It is quite easy for us to forget the extent to which biblical religion was originally non-scriptural. For much of the history of Israel, its faith was not rooted in a set of written texts at all, but in the encounter with the living God. Abraham was not confronted with a biblical text. In like manner, it was not a biblical text that was the agent of St. Paul's conversion; both Abraham and Paul were transformed by encounters with God.[7] The origins of the Bible are found in testimony, first oral and then written, to the saving work of God.

Modern Christianity's appeal to the authority of written texts distinguishes it from the biblical communities that produced the Scriptures. Those early communities bequeathed to us the Scriptures, they were not, by and large, governed by them. That both Augustine and Martin Luther would be converted by reading a text of the Bible demonstrates the fundamental difference between biblical religion and religion founded on the Bible. This insight can perhaps protect us against the temptation to look to the canon of the Bible as a depository of self-contained truths. The authority of the Bible cannot be sustained in this fashion. The authority of the Bible lies in its being a testimony to something prior, something beyond the written text; it is a testimony to the saving and revelatory action of God in history. This understanding of the Bible as testimony serves as an important corrective to that deadly tendency to turn the Bible into an "owner's manual," or to refer to the Bible itself as the "Word of God" without qualification. It is better, perhaps, to consider the Bible as *the inspired testimony* to the living Word of God encountered in history, by the power of the Spirit, from the beginning of time and, in "the fullness of time," in Jesus of Nazareth.

Contemporary Catholicism has learned much from the Churches of the Reformation, not the least of which being the importance of the Bible as offering foundational testimony for the Christian faith. However, Catholicism has generally rejected the classical Protestant view that the authority of the Bible precedes that of the Church. For Catholicism, the Bible is the product of the faith of Israel and the early Christian communities. On the other hand, Catholicism has sometimes abused this insight. Certain church attitudes and practices have sometimes given the impression that the chronological priority of Church over Bible justifies limiting the authority of the Bible to a kind of remote corroboration for the authoritative teaching of the pope and bishops. This view fails to do justice to the circularity of authority in the Church: under the guidance of the Spirit the Church authoritatively established the canon, but did so with the recognition that this canon would subsequently bind the teaching and practice of the Church.

Finally, we should point out that Scripture does not function solely to ground Christian faith in the past; it also orients Christianity toward the future. Our conventional way of understanding the Bible is to see it as giving historical testimony to what God *has* accomplished, and that is true. But the Bible also stands as a testimony to the future, to what God *wishes* to accomplish in the future. We must turn to the Bible to help us interpret our present experience in the light of the future promised us in faith, promises that appear throughout the Scriptures.[8] By promise and future, I do not mean "predictions" of future events as one often finds with fundamentalist readings of the book of Revelation. I mean the way in which the biblical texts give testimony to a world yet to be realized, a world of grace and mercy, a world in which "the lion shall lie down with the lamb" and in which "they shall beat their swords into ploughshares."

This discussion of the complex relationship between the authority of the Bible and the life of the Church leads us to the subject matter of the next chapter: the relationship between Scripture and tradition.

DISPUTED QUESTIONS

1) The different canons of the Old Testament continues to be a matter of scholarly debate. In the last forty years some Protestant scholars have been calling for a reassessment of the Protestant position on this matter. They have challenged their own traditions to consider the consequences of the fact that Luther's justification of a narrower canon seems to have been based on St. Jerome's erroneous assumption regarding the Jewish canon. On the other hand, Catholic scholars have brought to light some complexities involved in the Council of Trent's declaration of canonical books. They note the irony in Trent's having declared Jerome's Vulgate normative even though Jerome himself held for a shorter canon. They also point out the alarming lack of scholarly expertise brought to bear on the question by the council.

2) Just as feminist biblical scholarship has raised questions regarding patriarchal bias in the processes of biblical authorship, so too they have questioned whether patriarchal assumptions influenced early church decisions regarding the canonicity of certain texts. Did these cultural biases lead the early Christian community to exclude women's perspectives from the canon or to enshrine texts that promote the denigration of women? Some feminists accept the canon as provisionally normative but warn that one should not see the assertion of an authoritative biblical canon as a negative judgment on the spiritual value of other non-canonical texts from the biblical period, some of which cast women in a more positive light.

FOR FURTHER READING

Abraham, William J. *Canon and Criterion in Christian Theology.* Oxford: Clarendon Press, 1998.

Barr, James. *Holy Scripture: Canon, Authority, Criticism.* Philadelphia: Westminster, 1983.

_____. *The Scope and Authority of the Bible.* Philadelphia: Westminster, 1980.

Brown, Raymond E. and Raymond F. Collins. "Canonicity." In *The New Jerome Biblical Commentary,* Raymond E. Brown, Joseph A. Fitzmyer and Roland E. Murphy, eds., 1034–54. Englewood Cliffs, N.J.: Prentice Hall, 1990.

De Hamel, Christopher. *The Book. A History of the Bible.* London: Phaidon Press, 2001.

Fiorenza, Elisabeth Schüssler. *In Memory of Her: A Feminist Theological Reconstruction of Christian Origins.* New York: Crossroad, 1983.

Gnuse, Robert. *The Authority of the Bible: Theories of Inspiration, Revelation and the Canon of Scripture.* New York: Paulist, 1985.

Hagen, Kenneth, ed. *The Bible in the Churches: How Various Christians Interpret the Scriptures.* Milwaukee: Marquette University Press, 1998.

Lienhard, Joseph T. *The Bible, the Church, and Authority: The Canon of the Christian Bible in History and Theology.* Collegeville: The Liturgical Press, 1995.

Russell, Letty, ed. *Feminist Interpretation of the Bible*. Philadelphia: Westminster, 1985.

Schneiders, Sandra M. *The Revelatory Text: Interpreting the New Testament as Sacred Scripture*. New York: HarperCollins, 1991; Collegeville: The Liturgical Press, 1999.

Sundberg, Albert. "The Bible Canon and the Christian Doctrine of Inspiration," *Interpretation* (1974) 352–71.

THREE ══════════════════════════════════════

WHAT IS THE RELATIONSHIP
BETWEEN SCRIPTURE
AND TRADITION?

When Catholics think about Scripture and tradition, many conceive the relationship between these two as if there were a two-drawer filing cabinet holding all the "truths" of divine revelation. One drawer contains the truths found in the Bible, and this drawer is shared by all Christians. The second drawer, however, refers to another set of truths not explicitly found in the Bible. This drawer is tradition and it is thought to be in the exclusive possession of the Roman Catholic Church. This imaginary construct, though never enshrined in official Catholic teaching, dominated the Catholic consciousness for almost four hundred years. As we will see, the Second Vatican Council went a long way toward dismantling it.

The word "tradition" comes from the Latin verb, *tradere* and means "to pass or hand something on." When we think of tradition in this basic sense, as the process of handing on the faith, it becomes clear from our discussion in the last chapter that the Bible is itself the fruit of tradition. Before there were written texts there were stories that were "handed on" from generation to generation and community to community. If we understand tradition in this way, as the "handing on" of the good news of salvation, then tradition might be thought of as preceding and even giving rise to the Bible. In some sense, then the Bible is both the fruit of this "traditioning" process, and, in the post-biblical period, the vital reference point for any and all subsequent "handing on" of the faith.

41

In the early Church "tradition" had both the dynamic sense of the *process* of handing on the faith, and a more objective sense in which it represented that which was being handed on, the *content* of the apostolic faith. It is fair to say, in any event, that through most of the first thousand years of Christianity no one conceived of tradition as something completely separate from Scripture. Tradition was the faith of the Church testified to in Scripture and now preserved through the example of martyrs, the witness of ordinary believers, the celebration of the liturgy and sacraments, theological reflection and Christian art. Only in the Middle Ages does tradition begin to acquire a more independent status as a collection both of church teachings and customs.

The question of the proper theological relationship between Scripture and tradition did not arise until the Protestant Reformation and the Reformers' espousal of the *sola scriptura* doctrine. The Reformers objected to the haze of accumulated customs, practices and speculative propositions that had proliferated in late medieval Catholicism, all of which, in their view, clouded over and even distorted the evangelical message of the Bible. The first formal Catholic explanation of its own understanding of the relationship between Scripture and tradition came at the Council of Trent, largely in response to the Reformers. In one of its decrees the council tried to articulate the proper relationship between these two terms. An early draft proposed that divine truths were contained "partly" in the "written books" and "partly" in unwritten traditions (the Council of Trent did not refer to "tradition" in the singular). The final text, however, was changed to read that truth was found "both in the written books and in unwritten traditions." The first formulation suggested that these were two distinct sources of divine truth, yet the final formulation was at least open to the interpretation that there were not different *sources* of truth at all but only different *modes of expression*. Many theologians would, after the Reformation, maintain the view more reflective of the first formulation. In other words, with important exceptions (e.g., Bossuet, Möhler, Newman), many Catholic theologians would continue to hold the view that Scripture and tradition were distinct sources of revelation.

This view was indirectly strengthened in the nineteenth century. Popes Gregory XVI, Pius IX and Leo XIII greatly expanded the teaching office of the papacy. These three popes began to use encyclicals as a vehicle for delivering authoritative doctrinal pronouncements. In 1854 Pope Pius IX "solemnly defined" the dogma of the Immaculate

Conception. There is even a story that, during the First Vatican Council, Pius IX learned of the desire of some bishops to have the council affirm that the pope's teaching must be in accord with tradition. The pope is said to have retorted in exasperation, "tradition? *I am* tradition!" Whether this story is true or not, it reflects a then common view of the papacy as the principal "organ of tradition." This growing tendency to identify the magisterium in general, and the papacy in particular, with tradition, strengthened the sense that tradition was a source of divine truth entirely separate from Scripture.

VATICAN II ON SCRIPTURE AND TRADITION

In the decades prior to Vatican II many theologians began to challenge the dominant understanding of tradition at the time. They recognized that the schematization of Scripture and tradition as two different sources was foreign to the Christian heritage of the first thousand years. Indeed, they insisted that while the late medieval and baroque theologians would speak of "traditions" in the plural, there was a more ancient insight reflected in the use of "tradition" in the singular as a way of naming the whole of the Christian faith passed on from generation to generation. Individual customs and traditions served as concrete and particular expressions of the one great tradition. They also contended that it was unfaithful to the witness of the early Church to imagine that only the pope and bishops had responsibility for handing on the apostolic faith.

The preparatory draft on divine revelation, given to the bishops at the beginning of the council, ignored all of these developments. That document made the "two-source theory" the center piece of its theology of revelation. Many bishops roundly criticized the draft, noting that while theologians had often assumed the theory of two sources, it had never been proposed as the authoritative teaching of the Church. After a debate filled with accusation and intrigue, Pope John XXIII ordered that the entire preparatory document be removed and that an alternative document be drafted by a newly created mixed commission. That new draft, after undergoing considerable revision, would eventually reflect the fruit of the theological development that had emerged in the preceding decades.

Instead of two sources of divine revelation, the council wrote that Scripture and tradition "make up a single deposit of the word of God, which is entrusted to the church" (DV #10). Here the ancient unity of Scripture and tradition was restored. Perhaps most significant, how-ever, is the broader framework in which Scripture and tradition were considered. As I noted in the introduction, the Dogmatic Constitu-tion on Divine Revelation shifted away from a propositional view of divine revelation. When revelation was understood as a set of individ-ual truths, the two-source theory (the "two-drawer filing cabinet") made sense. However, once the council focused instead on revelation as the living Word incarnate as Jesus of Nazareth, it became possible to orient both Scripture and tradition as distinct but inter-related mediations of the same living Word. The council presented tradition as a dynamic, living reality:

> The tradition that comes from the apostles makes progress in the church, with the help of the holy Spirit. There is a growth in insight into the re-alities and words that are being passed on. This comes about through the contemplation and study of believers who ponder these things in their hearts. It comes from the intimate sense of spiritual realities which they experience. And it comes from the preaching of those who, on succeeding to the office of bishop, have received the sure charism of truth. Thus, as the centuries go by, the church is always advancing to-wards the plenitude of divine truth, until eventually the words of God are fulfilled in it (DV #8).

There is a wealth of insight in this brief passage. First, the council af-firmed that the pope and bishops were not the exclusive "organs of tradition." The passage does mention the indispensable role of the bishops, but not before it first cites the role of believers who, through contemplation, study and intimate experience, allow church tradition to "progress." Elsewhere the council will affirm the *sensus fidei,* the supernatural sense or instinct of the faith possessed by all believers through baptism:

> Through this sense of faith which is aroused and sustained by the Spirit of truth, the people of God, under the guidance of the sacred magiste-rium to which it is faithfully obedient, receives no longer the words of human beings but truly the word of God; it adheres indefectibly to "the faith which was once for all delivered to the saints"; it penetrates more deeply into that same faith through right judgment and applies it more fully to life (LG #12).

This supernatural sense of the faith is the means by which all the bap-tized contribute to the Church's corporate "listening" to God's Word.

Second, the "traditioning" process active in the life of the whole Church is grounded in the triune life of God and, in particular, the work of the Holy Spirit. If it is God who in the fullness of love "addresses us as friends," and it is Christ who is the "mediator and sum total of revelation (DV #2)," it is the Holy Spirit

> . . . who moves the heart and converts it to God, and opens the eyes of the mind and "makes it easy for all to accept and believe the truth." The same holy Spirit constantly perfects faith by his gifts, so that revelation may be more and more deeply understood (DV #5).

Attention to the Holy Spirit in the life of the Church has been one of the most overlooked contributions of the Second Vatican Council.

Finally, this passage reminds us that divine truth is not something that the Church ever really possesses. As befits a "pilgrim Church," the council modestly acknowledged only that the Church was "advancing towards the plenitude of divine truth." There is a kind of "eschatological humility" evident in this passage. It is one thing to say that the Church abides in the truth as it abides in God. It is altogether something different to say that the Church possesses the fullness of truth. According to the council, truth is never fully in the Church's possession this side of the Second Coming of Christ.

TRADITION: CONTINUITY AND DISCONTINUITY

Scripture and tradition are integrally related, proceeding as they do from the one Word of God, but they are not identical. Within the life of the Church, Scripture offers a kind of fixed point, a finite set of normative texts that grounds Christian faith in a set of ancient testimonies to foundational events: the Exodus and offer of God's covenant, God's saving deeds on behalf of Israel, Christ's life and ministry, death and resurrection. Tradition always embraces this scriptural testimony while going beyond it in bringing the Scriptures into critical dialogue with the life of the churches from generation to generation. New insights regarding the significance of biblical testimony for the community of faith "add to" tradition. The teaching of the Councils of Nicaea and Ephesus on the Trinity go beyond the biblical testimony even as the members of those councils would have insisted on their fidelity to Scripture. Consequently we must recognize that while tradition stands in "continuity" with the biblical testimony and shares a common source in the living Word of God, it is not strictly identical to it.

Tradition also bears witness to real discontinuities with the past. Any one with knowledge of the history of Catholic doctrine and practice knows that there are significant differences between the forms and manifestations of the Christian faith in the early centuries and those common today. John Thiel, in a recent study of the theology of tradition, offers a helpful framework for considering how an authentic view of tradition can hold together both a sense of continuity over time and a recognition of real change. He does this by following the medieval practice of considering four different "senses" of a biblical text. Thiel proposes that one can also identify four different "senses" of tradition.[1]

The "Literal" Sense of Tradition

The first "sense of tradition" is what Thiel calls the "literal sense." By this he means those beliefs and practices within the Christian tradition that have endured over long periods of history, give the impression of stability and are viewed as authoritative. The literal sense of tradition does not preclude any change in these beliefs and practices for, as with all beliefs and practices, there are bound to be variances in interpretation. Nevertheless, when we consider the literal sense of tradition, it is the sense of stability over time that is dominant. We can identify a number of core Christian teachings that, even allowing for variances in theological explanation, have been relatively stable throughout church history: the Christian hope for eternal life or the belief that Christ is fully human and fully divine. Such examples of the literal sense of tradition demonstrate that, although theological interpretations have varied, one can recognize enduring insight maintained across several Christian epochs.

The Sense of Tradition as Development-in-Continuity

Thiel's second sense of tradition is that of "development-in-continuity." Where the literal sense of tradition highlights those aspects of tradition that exhibit relatively little change over time, development-in-continuity highlights those aspects of tradition that do give evidence of significant growth and development. This sense was explicitly affirmed for the first time in an ecclesiastical document in Vatican II's *Dei Verbum* #8: "The tradition that comes from the apostles makes progress in the church, with the help of the holy Spirit. There is a growth in insight into the realities and words that are being passed on."

Although Vatican II offers the first official articulation of the dynamic growth and development of tradition, theories of how doctrine developed over time had been proposed in the nineteenth-century by important Catholic thinkers like Johann Adam Möhler and John Henry Newman. This was in part due to the nineteenth-century fascination with the metaphor of an organism that can mature while still preserving its fundamental identity. This sense of tradition assumes that while the fullness of divine revelation was given to the apostolic community, the full significance of this definitive revelation could only be "unpacked" over time in the life of the Church. "Ideas" given to the early Church are seen as unfolding gradually over time.

This second sense of tradition represents an important step beyond a kind of Catholic fundamentalism that focuses on pristine truths and practices thought to be immune to change of any kind. It recognizes the reality of change, but insists that such change occurs while preserving the essential identity of that which undergoes change. Tradition as development-in-continuity has played an important role in Catholic thought because it presents tradition from the perspective of divine providence; the change and development that occur do so by the invisible hand of God's Spirit at work in the Church from generation to generation. Many nineteenth-century thinkers assumed this perspective in their explanations of how the dogma of the Immaculate Conception achieved its developed expression in the nineteenth-century dogmatic definition of Pope Pius IX.

One obvious danger with this reading of tradition as continuity-in-development is the tendency to read history as if all development were moving easily and surely by God's hand to our present moment. We are inclined to read tradition from "God's perspective," as Thiel puts it. But of course, we do not and will never have access to history from "God's perspective." We are forced, whether we like it or not, to interpret history as historical beings ourselves. We have no privileged reading of history from some ethereal plane.

This suggests the need for caution in appealing to this sense of tradition. That God's hand is at work in the movement of tradition is assumed by all Catholic Christians. But our *recognition* of the work of God's hand is another matter entirely. We are tempted to imagine contemporary church teachings as having been invisibly and inexorably directed toward their present formulation. We stand at the present moment and look back on history, trying to recognize the movements of the Spirit. But our present perspective is always partial and to a considerable extent, it undergoes revision over time. What today strikes us as an obviously providential development of a given insight might conceivably, one hundred years from now, be viewed as a dead-end street. Up to the nineteenth century, many Christians saw slavery as part of God's divine plan. Today, Christians recognize this position for what it is: a tragic misreading of Divine Providence.

We do believe in faith that it is possible to recognize the hand of God, both in our own personal faith journeys, and in the history of the Church, but with rare exceptions (that we will address in a later chapter) this discernment is not infallible and is often open to revision. A personal example might demonstrate the point. If I had written a narrative ten years ago of how the Spirit of God had been guiding me in a variety of decisions that led me to marry my wife, Diana, and become a theologian, it would doubtless read quite differently from the narrative of those same events I would write today. Our corporate view of tradition can be understood in much the same way. We look back on our common history and read that history out of the questions and concerns of the present moment.

Thiel suggests that this "retrospective" approach actually does more justice to the history of doctrine than an attempt to adopt "God's view" of history. A good example is the dogma of the Immaculate Conception. The organic model of development tried to present this teaching as if it matured consistently and without interruption from the time of the New Testament to its eventual definition in 1854. Such a perspective has the disadvantage of having to stretch the historical data to fit the theory. In fact, it is quite difficult to see any early maturation in this dogma at all, particularly before Augustine's articulation of the doctrine of original sin. As late as the thirteenth century significant theologians like Thomas Aquinas were un-persuaded by this teaching. An honest reading of the history of this doctrine cannot produce a narrative of continuous and unswerving development. This need not deny the legitimacy of the teaching, however. It is quite possible to affirm that in 1854, *looking back on the history of Marian reflection*, the understanding of the Immaculate Conception emerged, not as a single progressive development, but by "fits and starts" such that only in the nineteenth century could the fragmentary and partial insights that were peppered through the history of Marian reflection be connected in such a way as to enable the dogmatic *recognition* of Mary's role in salvation history.

The Sense of Tradition as a Reversal of Past Beliefs and Practices

The first two senses recognize that at the present moment there is some insight, belief or practice identified within tradition that the believing community wishes to affirm. But this avoids a tricky question: what happens when the Church ceases to affirm an insight, belief or practice that had commonly been affirmed in the past? Tradition is not always the story of enduring or developing beliefs and practices; sometimes it is the story of beliefs and practices that have been abandoned or rejected over time. Tradition involves not only the recognition of continuities with the past, but sometimes the recognition of dramatic discontinuity and even the reversal of positions. Some beliefs and practices simply lose their authority over time. We mentioned earlier the sad truth that slavery was long viewed as an institution fully in accord with both natural law and divine revelation. The grudging rejection of this viewpoint in the consciousness of the Church can only be viewed as a communal recognition of dramatic *discontinuity* with its past. In a similar way the Church has found it necessary to repudiate longstanding beliefs about the immorality of charging interest when lending money, the inherent inferiority of women in the natural order and the denial of religious liberty to non-believers.

What distinguishes this sense of tradition from the previous two is that it is acknowledging not a sense of stability or continuity of belief and practice over time but rather a sense of dramatic discontinuity. Some theories have tried to gloss over such discontinuities by claiming that, if one looks deeply enough, there is a consistent affirmation evident underneath the appearance of change and repudiation. Efforts have been made, for example, to see in the Second Vatican Council's teaching on religious liberty and the universal reach of God's saving offer nothing more than new formulations of past insights. These insights may have been expressed imperfectly or in an underdeveloped manner, it is held, but they can be found in the tradition.

One senses a kind of historical dishonesty in such attempts, however. Perhaps it is more honest simply to recognize the general fallibility of the Church as a pilgrim people (regarding that which does not pertain directly to God's saving offer) that is moving toward the "fullness of truth," but is not protected from wrong turns along the way. Indeed, one way of thinking about the Church's teaching on the charism of infallibility and the irreversibility of certain of the Church's teachings, is to see the exercise of infallibility as an exceptional instance in which elements of church tradition, understood in the literal sense, are excluded from the possibility of dramatic reversal envisioned in this sense of tradition. How the Church comes to this infallible judgment will have to be considered in later chapters.

This third sense of tradition as reversal should not be thought of as a kind of failure of tradition or a negation of it. Tradition is sustained by the discernment of the whole Church regarding the integrity and authenticity of the received apostolic faith. That this discernment will, on occasion, yield a reversal is not a failure of tradition but the proof of its vitality.

The Sense of Tradition as Novel

If we are really to accept the dynamic character of tradition, we must see it as more than simply the preservation or development of the "old" but also as the openness to what appears as novel, provocative, prophetic. Authentic Christian tradition is never merely concerned with memory; it is also oriented toward the future. Tradition must draw us forward to the fulfillment of God's reign and that can only happen if, along with the affirmation of ancient and enduring beliefs and practices, there is a place in tradition for the new insight, practice or perspective that can serve to reinvigorate or reorient tradition. This brings us to Thiel's fourth sense of tradition as embracing the novel.

What we are considering here is the situation in which a new belief or practice is initially advocated by a small minority within the Church. Many elements of church tradition that we think of as enduring (and therefore as belonging to the literal sense of tradition) were originally presented by a minority and appeared to many as novel. Thiel reminds us that the Council of Nicaea's view that the Logos was "one in being with the Father," a belief that we now accept as an enduring feature of Christian tradition, was actually a minority position in the fourth century. At that time the majority of Christians accepted the views of the Alexandrian presbyter Arius, who insisted that the Logos was subordinate to the

Father within the Godhead. Though St. Athanasius and the bishops at the Council of Nicaea insisted that what they were teaching was in conformity with the ancient apostolic faith, many Christians undoubtedly viewed their unprecedented use of the Greek term *homoousios* (of the same being or substance), as a novelty. Indeed, it took over fifty years for the Nicene position to achieve widespread acceptance.

Unlike the first two senses of tradition, this fourth sense of tradition as novelty is inherently *unstable*. When something new is introduced into the life of the Church, such introductions are always tenuous and provisional. The "novelty" will either win wide acceptance over time and lose its novelty or it will eventually be dismissed. Canon law recognizes this dynamic when it notes that certain customs may legitimately arise within a community. If those customs endure for a significant amount of time, they gradually lose their status as custom and take on the force of law.

We must also note the way in which this sense of tradition often functions prophetically. Precisely because the novel perspective is initially voiced by a small number, there is a temptation to dismiss the novel as unfounded, trendy, politically correct or unbalanced. Yet often the new perspective calls the community to consider some hitherto unexamined aspect of the Christian life. Though the call to radical non-violence has been voiced throughout the Christian tradition, it has always had the character of the novel viewpoint, considered unrealistic or out of step with the classical tradition's embrace of Christian views of self-defense, just-war theory and the legitimate exercise of capital punishment. Yet the call to radical non-violence can also be viewed as prophetic, as calling believers to a vital yet neglected aspect of gospel living.

These four senses of tradition do not compete with one another. An authentic understanding of Catholic tradition must acknowledge the necessity of all four. Without the literal sense of tradition there would be no unity of Christian belief, no common profession of faith to unite believers. Without tradition as continuity-in-development, it would be impossible to recognize insights and practices whose "traditional" character only emerged over time. Finally without the senses of tradition as reversal and novelty, there would be no real change at all for both reversal and novelty are dynamisms that serve to expand, renew and revise the shared consciousness of the Christian faith. To hold these four senses of tradition together is to affirm with Pope John

XXIII that "the Church is not an archaeological museum, but is alive, tireless, and life-giving; and it makes its way forward, often in unexpected ways."[2]

DISPUTED QUESTIONS

1) The sense of tradition as a reversal or repudiation of past beliefs and practices is controversial. In the minds of some, this view challenges the belief that the Spirit, by Christ's promise, would always be with the Church protecting it from error—what theologians refer to as the "indefectibility" of the Church. They resist any admission of genuine reversals, preferring to view these so called "reversals" within a framework of development and growth. Others appeal to the possibility of reversal in tradition as they challenge certain contemporary church teachings.

2) The acceptance of the possibility of novelty within tradition can also be quite controversial. Feminist proposals regarding new images for naming God or new liturgical practices that emerge from grassroots practice (e.g., holding hands during the Lord's Prayer, use of liturgical dance) are often condemned as "untraditional." Theologians and church leaders can disagree on whether such novelty can be justified in a given instance. Some theologians would reject altogether the idea of novelty within the development of tradition, insisting instead that any legitimate "new" developments in tradition must emerge organically out of the old and not as the result of assimilating genuine novelty.

3) As we have seen, one of the really difficult questions in any theology of tradition has to do with how one relates continuity and change. A very common way to do this, offered by Pope John XXIII in his opening address at the council and frequently appealed to in the council documents themselves, is to make a distinction between form and content. One can affirm that the content or substance of a particular dogma remains unchanged even as its concrete articulation is subject to revision and reformulation. This is often called the "kernel and husk" theory of divine revelation where the kernel can clearly be distinguished from the exterior husk. As helpful as this distinction

has been, many theologians today question whether this kind of distinction is really adequate. They note the important ways in which the meaning of a dogma cannot be so easily separated or detached from the cultural, philosophical and theological forms that are used to express that meaning.

FOR FURTHER READING

Congar, Yves. "The Debate on the Question of the Relationship between Scripture and Tradition, from the Point of View of Their Material Content." In *A Theology Reader*. R. W. Gleason, ed. 115–29. New York: Macmillan, 1966.

_____. *The Meaning of Tradition*. New York: Hawthorn, 1964.

_____. *Tradition and Traditions: An Historical and Theological Essay*. New York: Macmillan, 1966.

Fiedler, Maureen and Linda Rabben, eds. *Rome Has Spoken . . .* New York: Crossroad, 1998.

Lash, Nicholas. *Change in Focus: A Study of Doctrinal Change and Continuity*. London: Sheed & Ward, 1973.

Mackey, J. P. *The Modern Theology of Tradition*. New York: Herder and Herder, 1963.

Meredith, Anthony. *Theology of Tradition*. Notre Dame: Fides, 1971.

Nichols, Aidan. *From Newman to Congar: The Idea of Doctrinal Development from the Victorians to the Second Vatican Council*. Edinburgh: T&T Clark, 1990.

O'Malley, John W. *Tradition and Transition: Historical Perspectives on Vatican II*. Wilmington, Del.: Glazier, 1988.

Thiel, John E. *Senses of Tradition: Continuity and Development in Catholic Faith*. New York: Oxford University Press, 2000.

Tilley, Terrence W. *Inventing Catholic Tradition*. Maryknoll, N.Y.: Orbis, 2000.

PART TWO

THE AUTHORITY OF
THE CHURCH'S
TEACHING OFFICE

FOUR

HOW DO WE UNDERSTAND
THE MAGISTERIUM TODAY?

Vatican II was the most important church event in the history of modern Catholicism. The council addressed such vital questions as the renewal of the liturgy, the Church's mission in the world, the role of the laity, the future of ecumenism, the importance of respectful dialogue with other world religions and the right of all people to religious liberty. The council also addressed important issues related to the nature and structure of the Church today. Although the council offered no systematic theology of the magisterium, its teaching has had a huge impact on contemporary understanding of the Church's teaching office.

THE TEACHING OF VATICAN II

When Vatican II opened in October 1962, it had been over ninety years since the last ecumenical council. The First Vatican Council met from 1869 to 1870. That council had planned to offer a comprehensive document on the Church, but it could only approve a document on the Catholic faith and another on the papacy before the council was suspended because of the Franco-Prussian war. After lively debate, the document on the papacy had solemnly defined the dogmas of papal primacy and papal infallibility. These definitions included important limits to papal authority. However, those limits were often little understood and, when combined with the council's inability to address the role of the bishops in any detail, the result was a strongly papo-centric vision of the Church that would continue until Vatican II.

The bishops at Vatican II set about redressing the imbalance created by Vatican I. At the beginning of the council, the bishops were given a preparatory draft on the Church that reflected the general tendencies of Catholic ecclesiology in the decades between the two councils. This document presented the Catholic Church as a visible, hierarchical institution identical with the Body of Christ on earth. The bishops ultimately rejected that draft as inadequate and their final document, the Dogmatic Constitution on the Church, *Lumen gentium,* offered a considerably different vision of the Church. Put in its simplest terms, the council recovered the properly *theological* foundations of the Church. The Church certainly was a visible institution, but its visibility was no longer understood exclusively through the lens of canon law. The Church's visible structures were not ends in themselves. The sacraments, church office, daily Christian witness, these were the visible elements of the Church that made the Church itself a sacrament of salvation in the world. The council described the Church as a spiritual communion of life and love that drew believers into communion with God in Christ by the power of the Holy Spirit. The bishops drew attention to the trinitarian foundations of the Church, quoting St. Cyprian who wrote that the Church was "a people made one by the unity of the Father, the Son and the holy Spirit" (LG #4).

In continuity with the teaching of Pius XII, the council offered a beautiful meditation on the Church as the Body of Christ, but it added to this a reflection on the role of the Holy Spirit "which dwells in the church and in the hearts of the faithful as in a temple." This Spirit "guides the church in the way of all truth and, uniting it in fellowship and ministry, bestows upon it different hierarchic and charismatic gifts, and in this way directs it and adorns it with his fruits" (LG #4). The council also decided to place a chapter on the Church as the new people of God in front of its chapter on the hierarchy. The message was clear. Before there could be any consideration of the unique ministry of the clergy, one must first acknowledge that all believers shared a common identity and equality by virtue of faith, baptism and the call to discipleship.

When the council turned to its consideration of ordained ministry in chapter three of *Lumen gentium,* it focused on reasserting the authority of the bishops, both as individual pastors and as belonging to a universal college that shared, with the bishop of Rome, responsibility for the welfare of all the churches. Vatican I had considered the role of the bishops largely in the context of the papacy. Vatican II, by contrast, began with consideration of the bishops. In its theological reflection on the ministry of the bishop, the council drew for inspiration on the practice of the early Church.

First, in article 21 of *Lumen gentium,* the council affirmed that the office of the bishop was not just the "highest degree" of the priesthood, but the fullness of the sacrament of holy orders. Following ancient practice, it is now the bishop, rather than the priest, who is the principal minister of the local church. The council also taught that episcopal power was communicated through episcopal ordination itself. The pope did not delegate power and authority to the bishops, though he could regulate episcopal jurisdiction. The bishop was more than a vicar of the pope. Article 27 stated that every bishop could rightly be called a "vicar of Christ." Regarding the nature of the bishop's pastoral responsibilities, the council wrote:

> The pastoral charge, that is, the permanent and daily care of their sheep, is completely entrusted to them fully; nor are they to be regarded as vicars of the Roman Pontiff; for they exercise a power which they possess in their own right and are most truly said to be at the head of the people whom they govern (LG #27).

Because the Gospel the bishop proclaims is not a secret Gospel but is the authoritative proclamation of the apostolic faith shared by the whole Church, the bishop must be an effective listener if he is to be an effective teacher. This is affirmed in *Lumen gentium*'s chapter on the laity:

> The laity should disclose their needs and desires to the pastors with that liberty and confidence which befits children of God and brothers and sisters in Christ. To the extent of their knowledge, competence or authority the laity are entitled, and indeed sometimes duty-bound, to express their opinion on matters which concern the good of the church (LG #37).

Of course, just as the bishop is not simply a mouthpiece for the pope, neither is he a mouthpiece for the opinions of his flock reflected in the latest poll. A "special charism of truth" is given to him, and it is his responsibility, and his alone, to exercise that charism faithfully. Although the bishop serves as a *testis fidei,* a witness to that faith which is professed by those in his community, he is also the authoritative teacher and judge of the faith (*iudex fidei*), responsible for safeguarding the faith from the distortion and error which is always possible within any individual community.

The council also addressed a topic almost completely overlooked by Vatican I, namely, the bishops' relationship to one another as a "college." The council taught that through episcopal ordination each bishop was inserted into the college of bishops (LG #22.1). It taught that the bishops, "together with their head, the Supreme Pontiff, and never apart from him . . . ," also ". . . have supreme and full authority over the universal church" (LG #22). In other words, the whole college of bishops shares, with the pope, in the pastoral care of the universal Church. By joining papal authority with the authority of the college of bishops, and recognizing that they share supreme and full authority over the Church, the council placed the papacy in a new, or more accurately, a more ancient ecclesiological context. Vatican II reaffirmed Vatican I's teaching on papal primacy and papal infallibility, but it situated these teachings within an ecclesial vision in which pope and bishops shared responsibility for the welfare of the whole Church. As we turn to consider the authority of the magisterium more explicitly in this second section, it will be important to keep in mind some basic theological principles regarding the nature of the Church and its teaching office.

NEGLECTED INSIGHTS INTO THE NATURE AND EXERCISE OF THE MAGISTERIUM IN THE CHURCH

The word *magisterium* means, literally, the authority of the master *(magister)* or teacher.[1] The term has a long and complicated history. It was used only infrequently in the early Church. In the late Middle Ages *magisterium* referred to the office and authority of teachers, both bishops and scholars. Thus St. Thomas Aquinas wrote of both the magisterium of the pastoral chair *(magisterium cathedrae pastoralis),* by which he meant the authority of the bishop, and the magisterium of the teaching chair *(magisterium cathedrae magistralis),* by which he meant the authority of the theologian. By the nineteenth century the meaning of the term *magisterium* had narrowed further. Now it was used almost exclusively in reference to, first the unique teaching authority of the bishops, and finally to the bishops themselves. Today the term is commonly used as a synonym for the college of bishops under the headship of the bishop of Rome.

The Church's teaching office has changed significantly over its two thousand years of existence. This has often produced some confusion.

Sometimes certain assumptions that were common in past ages still hold sway in the minds of many Catholics and non-Catholics alike. Although Vatican II made significant contributions, it offered no systematic treatment of the Church or church authority. Consequently, the implications of its vision are easily overlooked. It will be helpful to clarify some important and often neglected aspects of Catholic ecclesiology and their implications for our understanding of the magisterium.

The Church Is Not a Democracy . . . Neither Is It a Monarchy!

U.S. Catholics often approach their Church out of the particular assumptions of North American culture. Particularly here in the United States, our strong commitment to participative democracy leads us to expect the Church to function according to liberal democratic principles. Liberal democracies are built on the principle of one person-one vote wherein each person is expected to vote for their individual desires and preferences and the majority opinion assumes the force of law. Liberal democracies also presume that their leaders are nothing more than elected officials expected to represent the needs and desires of their constituents.

The Church is certainly not a democracy in this sense. It has a mission that was given to it by Christ. The Church is also a recipient of God's revelation. Consequently, its teaching must be determined, not by individual preferences, but by divine revelation itself. The Church's decisions are governed, not by changing opinion but by the determination to remain faithful to the message and mission it has received from Christ, in the Spirit. The Church is also not a democracy in the sense that it possesses a sacramentally constituted structure in which some from among the community are ordained for the unique ministry of ecclesial oversight *(episkope)* exercised by the bishop. They may be called forth by the community, but they are not representatives of the community in the sense of an elected functionary responsible for nothing more than communicating the will of the people. By virtue of their ordination bishops bear a special responsibility for the preservation of the apostolic faith of the Church.

Of course, just because the Church is not a liberal democracy, that does not mean that all democratic values and structures are antithetical to the nature and mission of the Church. Over its long history the Catholic Church has often incorporated democratic elements into its life. Bishops were elected in the early Church by the clergy and the people. Synods and councils have long employed participatory decision-making procedures. Since the eleventh century popes have been elected by the College of Cardinals. Men's and women's religious communities have often employed democratic structures in their choice of leadership and communal discernment. It follows that there is every reason to hope that further democratic elements might find their way into the life of the Church.

If the Church is not a liberal democracy, it is also not a monarchy or an aristocracy. Though many of the customs and titles associated with church leadership reflect a time when monarchical and aristocratic views of church leaders predominated (one still hears the cardinals referred to as "the princes of the Church"), these do not reflect the true nature of the Church.

In truth, the Church is neither a liberal democratic republic nor a papal monarchy; it is *sui generis*—an ordered spiritual communion. As such it *is*, however, a community of equals, a spiritual communion of persons in which all are called, by virtue of their baptism, to submit themselves to hear God's Word and discern God's will in the concrete circumstances of the community. This was affirmed in the teaching of Vatican II:

> Although by Christ's will some are appointed teachers, dispensers of the mysteries and pastors for the others, yet all the faithful enjoy a true equality with regard to the dignity and the activity which they share in the building up of the body of Christ. The distinction which the Lord has made between the sacred ministers and the rest of the people of God implies union, for the pastors and the other faithful are joined together by a close relationship. The pastors of the church, following the example of the Lord, should minister to each other and to the rest of the faithful; the latter should eagerly collaborate with the pastors and teachers. And so, amid their variety all bear witness to the wonderful unity in the body of Christ: this very diversity of graces, of ministries and of works gathers the children of God into one, for "all these things are the work of the one and the same Spirit" (LG #32).

How different this description of the Church is from that of Pius X who, five decades earlier, described the Church as an "unequal society . . . comprised of two ranks," the clergy, who are called to lead, and the laity who are called to follow! Since the Word of God is addressed to the whole Church, all Christians have, by virtue of their baptism, a vital role to play in discerning and handing on the Christian faith. Consequently, while bishops cannot be reduced to mere delegates of the community of the baptized, neither are they free to ignore the community of believers. Bishops must recognize that the faith of the Church abides in the life witness of all the faithful as much as in official church pronouncements. We will have more to say about this in Part Three on the authority of believers.

The Bishop Is "Vicar of Christ," Apostolic Leader of the Local Church He Serves

As Vatican II reminded us, the bishop is not a delegate of the pope but a true "vicar of Christ" (LG #27). His authority comes from episcopal ordination and his ministry is bound to the people he serves. His close relationship to his people is reflected in his ancient role as the principal presider over the Eucharist. Just as the presiding bishop gathers together and offers up the gifts and prayers of the community, so too the bishop as apostolic leader gathers up the faith insight of the whole community.

The early Church held together three basic convictions: (1) that the bishop was the apostolic leader of the local church; (2) that communion with him was a visible sign of communion in the Church; (3) that the bishop was not above the local church but bound to it as its pastoral leader. By the mid-third century St. Cyprian of Carthage had developed a very strong theology of the bishop's authority. To be united with Christ in the Church one had to be united with their bishop. At the same time, he believed that, precisely as their spiritual leader, the bishop was also accountable to his community. In a letter to his clergy, Cyprian wrote:

> . . . from the beginning of my episcopate, I decided to do nothing of my own opinion privately without your advice and the consent of the people. When I come to you through the grace of God, then we shall discuss in common either what has been done or what must be done concerning these matters, as our mutual honor demands.[2]

A century and a half later, yet another North African bishop, St. Augustine, expressed well the ancient conviction that the bishop was bound to his people in an intimate way:

bishops

> When I am frightened by what I am for you, then I am consoled by what I am with you. For you I am the bishop, with you I am a Christian. The first is an office, the second a grace; the first a danger, the second salvation.[3]

The spiritual bond between a bishop and his people was reflected in the early Church's prohibition against ordaining a bishop without a pastoral charge to a local church. To do so would turn episcopal ordination into an honorific rather than a call to serve a church. It was also commonly held that no bishop could be ordained for a local church without the consent of the people. Cyprian made this point well.

> Moreover, we can see that divine authority is also the source for the practice whereby bishops are chosen in the presence of the laity and before the eyes of all, and they are judged as being suitable and worthy after public scrutiny and testimony.[4]

The spiritual bond between bishop and people was often expressed in marital imagery. The bishop was, in a sense, "married" to his local church. Consequently, bishops were prohibited from transferring from one diocese to another.

Any consideration of episcopal teaching authority must hold together both the Catholic conviction regarding the authority the bishop possesses by virtue of his office and his integral relationship to the local church he serves.

The Assistance of the Holy Spirit Works through Human Processes

Catholicism holds that the bishops receive, by virtue of episcopal ordination, a special assistance of the Holy Spirit in the exercise of their teaching office. According to Richard McCormick, two extremes must be avoided.[5] The first extreme would be to subscribe to a kind of rationalism that refused to acknowledge any real influence of the Spirit on human action in general, and the exercise of the bishops' teaching office in particular. Catholics hold that there is a distinct "charism for truth" that is given to the bishops that distinguishes their ministry from that of other believers.

The second extreme would imagine the Holy Spirit working in a quasi-magical fashion, beyond the realm of human inquiry and judgment. For those who hold this view a bishop's possible lack of education or his unwillingness to listen to others would be irrelevant to the effectiveness of his teaching ministry because the bishop is given a unique assistance of the Holy Spirit. Those who subscribe to this view tend to downplay human factors in the exercise of the Church's teaching office. Karl Rahner observed that this approach to the assistance of the Holy Spirit assumes that the Holy Spirit intervenes "only at that point at which human efforts are suspended. In reality, however, God works precisely in and through these human efforts and his activity does not constitute a distinct factor apart from this."[6] To assert God's divine assistance it is not necessary, nor is it theologically sound, to assume that human processes are somehow suspended. We encountered this difficulty earlier when addressing the role of the Holy Spirit in the inspiration of the biblical authors. The assistance of the Holy Spirit need not be seen as an independent force overlaid on top of human effort, but as the Holy Spirit acting within and through genuine human effort. Vatican II acknowledged this when the council wrote of the magisterium's exercise of its teaching office:

> The Roman Pontiff and the bishops, in virtue of their office and because of the seriousness of the matter, are assiduous in examining this revelation by every suitable means and in expressing it properly. . . . (LG #25)

But what are the "suitable means" by which the pope and bishops engage in this investigation?

McCormick divides the relevant human processes into two categories: *evidence gathering* and *evidence assessing.* Evidence gathering refers to the many ways in which the human person inquires after the truth through study, consultation and investigation. With respect to the exercise of the Church's teaching office, this would involve a prayerful study of the Church's tradition (giving primacy of place to the testimony of Scripture), a consultation of scholars and theologians (representing diverse schools of thought and theological/historical perspectives), a consideration of the insights of pertinent related fields (e.g., the contributions of the social sciences or genetics), and an attempt to discern the sense of the faithful in and through whom the Spirit also speaks. Insufficient attention to this evidence-gathering can hamper the activity of the Spirit in bringing forth wisdom and insight through the bishops' teaching. Evidence assessing involves the proper consideration and assessment of the "evidence" gathered. Here again recourse to a diversity of theological scholarship will be important, but so will patient reflection and authentic conversation in contexts where the free exchange of views is clearly welcomed.

Catholics rely on the confidence that the assistance of the Holy Spirit brings, but this must not become an excuse for the Church's official teachers to shirk their responsibility to use the human resources at their disposal in the exercise of their teaching office.

The Church Is an Ordered Communion of Communions

Some Catholics today still hold to monarchical conceptions of the Church that suggest one vast, monolithic institution. They imagine a vertical chain of command moving from the laity up through the priests and bishops to the pope, who stands, as it were, at the apex of a great ecclesiastical pyramid. Popular though it may be, this view cannot be sustained theologically. If we are to grasp something of the nature of the Church we must look to its sacramental constitution. There we discover that the Church is first constituted by baptismal initiation into a community of disciples. The community of the baptized gathers together at the Sunday liturgy to be nourished in the life of communion. As such, the eucharistic liturgy represents the "summit and font" of the Christian life, sacramentally drawing believers into a spiritual communion that exists on many levels: (1) communion with God in Christ by the power of the Spirit, (2) communion with the fellow believers gathered at the eucharistic assembly, (3) communion with other eucharistic communities throughout the world, (4) communion with Christians who supped at the Lord's table in times past and (5) communion with the saints who celebrate at the eternal banquet.

This vision of the Church as a sacramental communion finds support in the New Testament understanding of *koinonia,* which is usually translated as "fellowship," "communion" or "participation." The biblical authors employed the word *koinonia* primarily to describe humankind's participation in the divine life of God. At the same time, however, *koinonia* also expressed the fellowship among Christians within the Body of Christ. The term *koinonia* articulated the fundamental connection between participation in the life of God and participation in Christian community. St. Paul's whole ecclesiology presupposed an organic view of the Church that suggested not just complementarity and diversity within the Church but *coexistence*.[7] For Paul, life in Christ meant life in the Body of Christ, the Church. The Church was no mere group of individuals. Rather, by baptism into the Christian community one participated in a new reality, one was a new creation. Individual believers did not *make* the Church, initiation into the Church through faith and baptism *made* the believer. For St. Paul, the celebration of the Eucharist was the most profound sacramental expression of this twofold *koinonia*. He writes:

> The cup of blessing that we bless, is it not a participation (*koinonia*) in the blood of Christ? The bread that we break, is it not participation (*koinonia*) in the body of Christ? Because the loaf of bread is one, we, though many, are one body, for we all partake of the one loaf (1 Cor 10:16-7).

In the early second century this biblical notion of *koinonia* or communion was extended to describe that spiritual bond that existed among all local eucharistic communities, past and present, as well as that bond that existed with the saints in heaven. There was a common conviction that all eucharistic communities were bound together in shared ecclesial communion. For the early Church the sacrament of the Eucharist brought about not only the communion of those gathered at each altar, but the communion of all local churches. This followed from the emerging eucharistic theology of the time. Wherever the Eucharist was celebrated, the Body of Christ was made sacramentally present. But the Body of Christ is one and cannot be fragmented. Therefore one must be able to speak of a unity, a communion, existing among all eucharistic communities. The one Church, Christ's Body, is actualized wherever believers gather for the breaking of the bread.

Each local church that hears God's Word proclaimed and celebrates the Eucharist under the presidency of an apostolic minister is more than a mere subdivision of the universal Church—it is truly the Body of Christ *in that place*. As the great ecumenist Jean von Allmen put it, each local church is "wholly the church, but not the whole church."[8] Since each church is truly Christ's Body in that place, each church stands as well in spiritual communion with every other eucharistic community. This relationship among the churches is no mere federation created by mutual contract; it is a profound spiritual communion sustained by the Holy Spirit. At the same time the eucharistic identity of each church prevents it from being subsumed into some larger whole.

Something of this vision of the Church as a communion of churches is reflected in the following diagram:

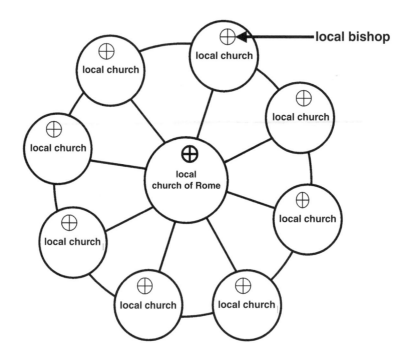

Each local church maintains its own integrity even as it stands in spiritual communion with other churches.

The Authority of the College of Bishops Is Grounded in the Universal Communion of Churches

When we conceive of the universal Church, not as a huge monolith but as an ordered communion of communions, we find a new framework for understanding the college of bishops. Each bishop is both pastor of a local church and member of the college of bishops. As such the bishop bears a twofold responsibility: (1) he must sustain and nourish the spiritual communion of the local church to which he is charged, preserving it in the apostolic faith, (2) he is called to extend, celebrate and nourish the communion that exists between his own church and the other local churches. The college of bishops is no external governing board standing above the Church. The college of bishops is *the visible expression* of the communion of churches and can never be separated from it. When the bishops gather in an ecumenical council, they are not participating in some extraordinary juridical event outside the life of the Church, they are offering a visible expression of what the Church in fact always is, a communion of communions.

One fruitful perspective on the college of bishops is to consider the episcopal interaction within the college as a kind of ecclesial "gift exchange."[9] Through his participation in the college of bishops each bishop offers the wisdom of his community—that unique inculturation of the one Gospel of Jesus Christ in his particular church—to the universal communion of churches. Each shares the insights and challenges that are experienced within his church and receives from the other bishops the gift of their churches' faith testimonies. As such, the ministry of the college of bishops always emerges out of and returns to the communion of the churches.

As Bishop of Rome the Pope Is Head of the College of Bishops

The pope is neither head of the whole Church, nor bishop of the whole Church. It is Christ and not the bishop of Rome who is head of the Church (cf. Eph 1:22-3; Col 1:18). Failure to preserve this basic biblical truth is, in part, what paved the way for the monarchical view of the Church discussed above. Neither is the pope the bishop of the universal Church. There is no such thing as a bishop of the universal Church. Every bishop is bishop of a local church.

It is worthwhile to remember that papal election is not a sacrament. That is, one is not ordained pope. The pope is pope only because he is first the bishop of the local church of Rome, a church which from ancient times was granted a distinctive primacy among all the churches. When the church of Jerusalem died out near the end of the first century, Rome supplanted Jerusalem as Christianity's "mother church." The Roman church was granted a certain priority among the churches in virtue of the tradition that it had received the apostolic teaching of, not one, but two apostles, Sts. Peter and Paul. At the beginning of the second century, St. Ignatius of Antioch would refer to Rome as the church "foremost in love"[10] and by the end of the same century St. Irenaeus of Lyons would refer to it as the church "of most excellent origins."[11] The authority of the church of Rome was gradually extended to its bishop. By the middle of the third century, the pope's authority as bishop of Rome was being grounded in the unique authority that Christ gave to St. Peter. Rome was viewed as a court of final appeal in disputes among the churches. In the fifth century the bishop of Rome began to exert his authority over the whole church (though the scope of his authority was much disputed in the East).

The unique pastoral responsibilities and authority of the pope today are still grounded in his ministry as bishop of Rome. Vatican I taught that it was in his capacity as bishop of Rome that the pope possesses a unique responsibility to preserve and nurture the unity of the faith and the communion of churches. All papal prerogatives, rightly understood, flow from this Catholic conviction.

If the pope is not head of the Church nor bishop of the whole Church, he is the *pastor* of the universal Church by virtue of his role as bishop of the local church of Rome. Moreover, he is head of the college of bishops as a member of that college. Vatican II taught that it is to the whole college of bishops, always under the headship of the bishop of Rome, that supreme power and authority was given to seek after the welfare of the Church. As head and member of this college, the pope can never be separated and opposed to the bishops. At the same time, neither can the bishops be constituted as a college without being in communion with the bishop of Rome.

Many theologians now believe that all significant papal actions exercised for the good of the whole Church are, by definition, collegial. This collegiality is made explicit when a pope convenes and presides over an ecumenical council. Yet, they would contend, even when the pope acts "alone," he does so as head of the college of bishops. His role as head of the college presumes that he is maintaining an informed communion with all the bishops. That communion with the bishops underlies all papal actions. Certainly, Vatican I taught that a pope cannot be legally bound to consult the bishops either before or after a solemn papal definition. At the same time, it is generally accepted today (and it was the opinion of many of the bishops at Vatican I), that the pope is still *morally* bound to engage in such consultation. Vatican I did not wish to place juridical limits on effective papal action. At the same time the council clearly presumed the pope would always act in communion with his brother bishops. To fail to consult the bishops would suggest a failure of the pope's responsibility as head of the college to preserve the unity of the college.

Pope John Paul II's encyclical on ecumenism, *Ut unum sint,* further developed the council's insights. In that encyclical he avoids traditional papal titles like "vicar of Christ," or "sovereign pontiff," preferring instead the title "bishop of Rome," and, even more profoundly, "the servant of the servants of God." The pope offers a vision of the papacy that goes far beyond that popularly associated with Vatican I. He presents the papacy as a ministry of service within the context of an ecclesiology of communion. Seen from this perspective, the Church is neither a federation of autonomous congregations nor a universal corporation with branch offices throughout the world. As a communion of churches, the pope insists that the primary responsibility for shepherding a local flock lies with the local bishop, the ordinary pastor of the local church. Extraordinary circumstances may require the pope to intervene in the affairs of a local church for the sake of the unity of faith and communion of all the churches. However, the principal exercise of papal primacy will be to support the bishops in the fulfillment of their pastoral ministry. The pope writes:

> The mission of the bishop of Rome within the college of all the pastors consists precisely in "keeping watch" (*episkopein*), like a sentinel, so that through the efforts of the pastors the true voice of Christ the shepherd may be heard in all the particular churches. . . . All this, however, must always be done in communion. When the Catholic Church affirms that the office of the bishop of Rome corresponds to the will of Christ, she does not separate this office from the mission entrusted to the whole body of bishops, who are also "vicars and ambassadors of Christ." The bishop of Rome is a member of the "college," and the bishops are his brothers in the ministry (UUS #s 94–95).

In this encyclical the pope offered an important advance, or perhaps more accurately, an important return, to a more ancient ecclesial vision of the papacy in service of the churches. It is an approach, I believe, that offers considerable ecumenical promise.

Today we are some four decades removed from the Second Vatican Council, and yet there is a wide recognition that the Church has much more to do if it wishes to fulfill the council's bold vision. The theological underpinnings the council offered for a new vision of church teaching authority have yet to be fully implemented. There can be no turning back from the path the council set for the Church of the future.

The work of the Church for decades to come will be to fulfill fearlessly and faithfully the council's vision of the Church as the Body of Christ, the pilgrim people of God, gifted by the Spirit, and sent in mission into the world to be a sacrament of God's saving offer.

DISPUTED QUESTIONS

1) Theological appeals to the Church as communion are not without controversy. There are, in fact, a number of competing versions of "communion-ecclesiology." Some theologians appeal to the theological category of "communion" in support of increased papal centralization while others appeal to the same theological concept as a justification for greater autonomy for the local churches. Consequently, we must be wary of any tendency to use communion ecclesiology to represent a superficial theological consensus or as a theological sleight-of-hand to dodge important ecclesiological disputes.

2) The view of the Church as a communion of churches and the fundamental identity of the bishop as spiritual leader of a local church has led some church critics to question the practice of ordaining titular bishops who are given "title" to a church which no longer exists while serving either as an auxiliary bishop in a large diocese, or as a church bureaucrat or diplomat. Critics of this practice argue that when bishops exercise their ministry without any real pastoral charge to an existing local church, the impression can easily be given that the office of bishop has become an honorific, a rank or title given to enhance an individual's prestige, rather than a ministry in service to a local church. These critics are convinced that the practice of giving a bishop title to a non-existent church trivializes the ancient conviction regarding the bishop's vital relationship to a genuine community of faith. They suggest that representatives of the Church engaging in diplomatic work around the world or functioning as bureaucrats within the Vatican need not be ordained bishop in order to fulfill their assigned tasks.

3) Born in the twelfth century as a kind of papal court for an imperial papacy, the Roman Curia has functioned for nine centuries as the bureaucratic arm of the papacy. It has provided

valuable service but, in the minds of many, it has also been remarkably resistant to reform. According to Vatican II, the Curia was to serve the pope and the bishops in the exercise of their pastoral ministry on behalf of the universal Church (CD #9). Many critics suggest that, rather than serving the bishops, the Curia has taken on the responsibility of "policing" the local churches, often asserting its will over against the legitimate pastoral prerogatives of local bishops. Defenders of the Curia note that many reforms of the Curia have indeed been undertaken in the last fifty years. The Curia has become much more international in its membership and a significant effort has been made to incorporate residential bishops into the various Roman dicasteries or congregations.

FOR FURTHER READING

Bianchi, Eugene C., and Rosemary Radford Ruether, eds. *A Democratic Catholic Church: The Reconstruction of Roman Catholicism.* New York: Crossroad, 1992.

Doyle, Dennis M. *Communion Ecclesiology: Vision and Versions.* Maryknoll, N.Y.: Orbis, 2000.

Gaillardetz, Richard R. Chapters 1 and 2 of *Teaching with Authority: A Theology of the Magisterium in the Church,* 3–65. Collegeville: The Liturgical Press, 1997.

Granfield, Patrick. *The Limits of the Papacy.* New York: Crossroad, 1987.

Mannion, Gerard, Richard Gaillardetz, Jan Kerkhofs and Kenneth Wilson, eds. *Readings in Church Authority: Gifts and Challenges for Contemporary Catholicism.* London: Ashgate, 2003.

Reese, Thomas. *Inside the Vatican: The Politics and Organization of the Catholic Church.* Cambridge: Harvard University Press, 1996.

Sullivan, Francis A. *Creative Fidelity: Weighing and Interpreting Documents of the Magisterium.* New York: Paulist, 1996.

_____. *Magisterium: Teaching Office in the Catholic Church.* New York: Paulist, 1983.

Tillard, Jean-Marie. *Church of Churches: An Ecclesiology of Communion.* Collegeville: The Liturgical Press, 1992.

FIVE

HOW DO THE POPE AND BISHOPS EXERCISE THEIR TEACHING AUTHORITY?

On Saturday you get up to read your daily newspaper over a cup of coffee, and in the religion section you read that your local bishop has just issued a pastoral letter on local immigration policy. A week later, you are watching the evening news and learn that the pope is planning a new encyclical on Catholic just-war teaching. Another week goes by and you receive the copy of your diocesan newspaper that reports that some Vatican congregation has issued a new document on the recruitment and training of seminarians. A few weeks later your pastor mentions in his homily a recent letter from the U.S. bishops' conference on devotion to Mary and the saints. Each of these represents, in some sense, an official exercise of the Church's teaching authority.

One can view this proliferation of church documents as an opportunity for adult education, but it has also become a source of great confusion. How do Catholics assess the significance of these different documents? Surely they are not all equally authoritative?

This is a difficult and, frankly, unprecedented issue. Catholics today are inundated with a number and variety of official church pronouncements unknown to previous generations. Consequently, Catholics today need assistance in sorting through the plethora of church documents to which they are exposed. This chapter will consider the ways in which this teaching office exercises its authority. One key for assessing the authoritative character of a church document is to look at who proposed it (e.g., an individual bishop, a bishops' conference, an ecumenical council, the pope) and the context in which it was proposed.

This will be the subject matter of this chapter. In the next chapter we will consider church teaching itself, exploring different categories of dogma, doctrine and church discipline.

An elaborate set of distinctions regarding the exercise of the magisterium has emerged out of the two-thousand year history of the Catholic Church. At the most general level we can distinguish between three distinct modes in which the Church's teaching office exercises its authority: (1) *the ordinary magisterium* refers to the more common exercises of the pope and bishops' teaching authority when they teach either individually or in groups; (2) *the extraordinary magisterium* refers to the more rare exercise of the Church's teaching office in the form of a solemn definition by either the pope or an ecumenical council; (3) *the ordinary universal magisterium* refers to the common judgment of the whole college of bishops (in union with the bishop of Rome) that a teaching is to be held as definitive. The following chart illustrates these distinctions.

THE EXERCISE OF THE MAGISTERIUM

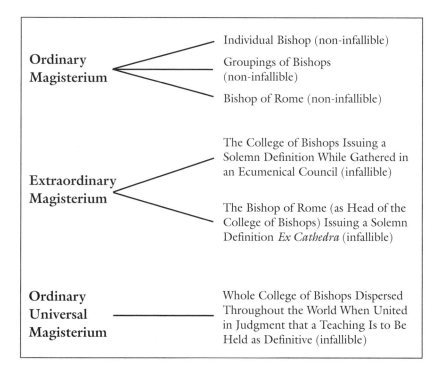

Ordinary Magisterium	Individual Bishop (non-infallible)
	Groupings of Bishops (non-infallible)
	Bishop of Rome (non-infallible)
Extraordinary Magisterium	The College of Bishops Issuing a Solemn Definition While Gathered in an Ecumenical Council (infallible)
	The Bishop of Rome (as Head of the College of Bishops) Issuing a Solemn Definition *Ex Cathedra* (infallible)
Ordinary Universal Magisterium	Whole College of Bishops Dispersed Throughout the World When United in Judgment that a Teaching Is to Be Held as Definitive (infallible)

THE ORDINARY MAGISTERIUM

The ordinary magisterium refers to the many different ways in which the pope and bishops, either individually or in groups, can teach authoritatively. Let us begin with the individual bishop.

The Teaching Office of the Individual Bishop

The Second Vatican Council considered the pastoral teaching office of the bishop in several texts.[1] *Lumen gentium* describes this teaching office:

> Among the more important duties of bishops, that of preaching the Gospel has pride of place. For the bishops are the heralds of the faith, who draw new disciples to Christ; they are authentic teachers, that is, teachers endowed with the authority of Christ, who preach to the people assigned to them the faith which is to be believed and applied in practice; and under the light of the holy Spirit they cause that faith to radiate, drawing from the storehouse of revelation new things and old; they make it bear fruit and they vigilantly ward off whatever errors threaten their flock (LG #25).

In the Decree on the Pastoral Office of Bishops, *Christus Dominus,* #12, the council notes that "in the exercise of their teaching office, [the bishops] are to proclaim to humanity the gospel of Christ. This is one of their principal duties."

Individual bishops exercise their teaching ministry in any of a variety of ways. The bishop is the chief evangelist and chief catechist in the local church. He must oversee the preaching and catechetical ministry of the church and ensure that through that ministry all within the local church hear of God's saving offer. The bishop himself will perform his catechetical ministry in his own preaching and catechesis and in the publication of pastoral letters and other ecclesiastical directives. Beyond his direct ministry of preaching and teaching, the bishop is further charged with safeguarding the authentic exposition of church teaching as that ministry is carried out by others within the local church. This means that his responsibility as teacher will include overseeing the catechetical work that takes place within his diocese.

Bishops who are effective teachers always do more than merely reiterate "official church teaching." As Vatican II taught, the bishop is more than a spokesperson for the pope. His teaching should, ideally, illuminate for his people the profundity of the Catholic tradition. The bishop must aspire to advance the cause of the faith through a prayerful and informed presentation of the Catholic tradition that does not simply repeat past formulations but seeks to bring new insight to church teaching. The bishop need not be a professional theologian but general theological competency and a thorough knowledge of the Christian tradition in its breadth and depth will be important for the effective fulfillment of his teaching ministry.

Frequently bishops will feel compelled to address complicated and sometimes controversial questions regarding the accepted teaching of the Church as it applies to a particular pastoral situation. This is particularly true with respect to the Church's moral teaching, where a bishop may need to make concrete moral determinations regarding particular questions and issues arising within a local church. One can easily imagine an individual bishop addressing a wide range of issues concerning immigration or welfare policy, the distribution of contraceptive devices in public schools, etc.

More rare will be those instances when a bishop will find it necessary to make a formal pronouncement on a doctrinal matter. When a bishop makes a formal doctrinal judgment, he does so specifically with the intent of proclaiming church doctrine in an authoritative and normative manner. When they teach individually, bishops do not exercise the charism of infallibility. However, they still teach authoritatively and the members of their local church have an obligation always to attend carefully and respectfully to their bishop's teaching. We will have more to say about this process in chapter 9.

The Teaching Authority of Synods and Episcopal Conferences

In the ancient Church it was common for bishops to meet in regional synods to deliberate on matters of common concern. Frequently these synods concerned themselves with pastoral and disciplinary matters, but on occasion more central doctrinal matters were also engaged. Some of Christianity's most central teachings first emerged out of such regional synods. These synods were considered genuine if partial expressions of episcopal collegiality. They were also practical examples of what would later be called the principle of subsidiarity, which, put simply, holds that local issues are best dealt with at the local level. A "higher authority" should intervene only when an issue cannot be resolved at the local level or when the welfare of the larger body is at stake.

Today such regional gatherings of bishops are relatively rare. However, in 1965, in response to several requests from bishops attending the Second Vatican Council, Pope Paul VI established the World Synod of Bishops, a consultative gathering of representative bishops from throughout the world to address a particular topic. Such synods, when meeting on a regular schedule, are called "ordinary synods." Additionally, the pope may call an "extraordinary synod" to address an issue of particular importance. In 1985 Pope John Paul II convened just such a synod to celebrate the twentieth anniversary of the close of Vatican II and to assess the reception of the council's teaching.

A modern alternative to the common practice of regional synods is the episcopal conference, an organization of bishops of a particular region or nation in order to address regional or national church issues. Episcopal conferences, as we know them today, first emerged in the early nineteenth century. These structures have long been accepted in the Church for their practical pastoral value.

Vatican II affirmed their value, and indeed, granted considerable authority to them. In the council's Constitution on the Sacred Liturgy, *Sacrosanctum concilium,* the council granted to episcopal conferences significant authority over a variety of liturgical matters (SC #22, 36, 39). In *Lumen gentium,* after discussing the ecclesial significance of the ancient patriarchal churches, the council affirmed that "in like fashion, the episcopal conferences at the present time are in a position to contribute in many and fruitful ways to the concrete realization of the collegiate spirit (LG #23)." The Decree on the Pastoral Office of the Bishop, *Christus Dominus,* also outlined the value and significance of episcopal conferences (CD #37–8).

In the 1980s the U.S. Bishops' Conference issued several significant pastoral letters, first on war and peace and then on the economy. These documents were viewed as prophetic by some and troubling by others. During this same period, questions were being raised by Vatican officials regarding the nature and limits of the teaching authority of bishops' conferences. Some defenders of the teaching authority of conferences noted that they were structurally equivalent to the regional synods of ancient times, synods that clearly exercised a real if limited doctrinal teaching authority. Others complained that Vatican II's teaching on collegiality affirmed the shared authority of the *whole* college of bishops, but not individual groupings of bishops. The crucial question concerned whether there could be intermediate exercises of episcopal authority between the authority of the individual bishop and the authority of the whole college.

Decades of debate led finally to Pope John Paul II's *motu proprio* (a document issuing at the pope's own initiative) *Apostolos suos,* issued in 1998. In that document the pope offered an historical survey of the development of episcopal conferences. He praised their contributions to the life of the Church and confirmed the limited doctrinal authority of episcopal conferences. The pope stipulated that episcopal conferences can issue binding doctrinal statements when (1) they issue the document in a plenary session (not by way of a committee), (2) the document is approved unanimously, or (3) the document is approved by a two-thirds majority and receives a *recognitio* (formal approval) from Rome. Under these conditions the teaching of episcopal conferences becomes a legitimate exercise of the ordinary magisterium.

The Ordinary Papal Magisterium

Just as individual bishops and groupings of bishops such as episcopal conferences can share in the Church's ordinary magisterium so too the pope exercises an ordinary teaching authority referred to as the ordinary *papal* magisterium. This teaching, which can take many forms, is a concrete expression of his unique ministry to stand watch over the faith of the universal Church.

Popes have claimed doctrinal authority on matters of faith and morals, going back to the first centuries of Christianity. However, they actually exercised that authority only infrequently. In the Middle Ages it was more common for popes to delegate thorny doctrinal or theological questions to the distinguished theology faculties of the great medieval universities like that found in Paris. When popes felt compelled to pronounce on doctrinal questions, these pronouncements were relatively terse and to the point. This began to change in the nineteenth century, largely through the use of the papal encyclical as a medium for papal teaching.

The papal encyclical itself was a relatively modern development, first employed in the eighteenth century by Pope Benedict XIV (1740–1758). However, his encyclicals were all very brief and largely either disciplinary or exhortatory in character. In the nineteenth century

Popes Gregory XVI (1831–1846) and Pius IX (1846–1878) made use of the encyclical, often addressing doctrinal matters, but these too were generally short in length. When they condemned erroneous views, there was no intention of stimulating new theological insight.[2] This changed with Pope Leo XIII (1878–1903), who issued such noteworthy encyclicals as *Aeterni patris, Providentissimus Deus, Satis cognitum* and *Rerum novarum*. The pontificate of Leo XIII marked the beginning of a modern development in the papacy in which popes began to offer, as part of their teaching ministry, extended theological treatments issued in magisterial documents on important topics. Pius X (1903–1914) would follow Leo's precedent with *Pascendi*, his encyclical condemning modernism, and both Popes Pius XI (1922–1939) and Pius XII (1939–1958) would issue lengthy encyclicals during their successive pontificates. This practice continued as well under Popes John XXIII and Paul VI. Perhaps more than any other pope in history, Pope John Paul II has used papal encyclicals, along with other ecclesiastical documents, to exercise his unique teaching ministry.

Popes today may exercise their ordinary teaching ministry through the issuance of various kinds of ecclesiastical documents. The chart below mentions a few of these.

Encyclical Letter: Documents offered by the pope as part of his ordinary magisterium and addressed to: (a) the whole college of bishops, (b) the whole Church or (c) the whole world. Encyclicals frequently address doctrinal/theological matters, but are not normally used to define dogma

Apostolic Letter: Papal letters usually sent to some particular category of persons, e.g., a group of bishops

Apostolic Exhortation: Documents issued by the pope in response to the deliberations of an episcopal synod

Occasional Papal Addresses: Speeches given to various groups who are received by the pope in the Vatican as well as speeches the pope gives on his travels

---

Although these are the main media by which the pope exercises his ordinary teaching office, popes do issue many other kinds of documents that are not normally doctrinal in character (e.g., an apostolic constitution or *motu proprio*). The publication of any of these documents might constitute an exercise of the ordinary papal magisterium, with, however, varying degrees of authority. One would expect, for example, that a new doctrinal formulation appearing in an encyclical would carry more weight than that offered in a weekly papal address. The teachings that are issued by way of the ordinary papal magisterium represent official church teaching and call for an internal assent by all Catholics (what exactly this means will be discussed in chapter 8). At the same time it must be noted that the ordinary papal magisterium does not engage the charism of infallibility.

THE EXTRAORDINARY MAGISTERIUM

One of the most controversial, and frankly, misunderstood teachings in Roman Catholicism is its teaching on infallibility. In order to grasp this teaching we need to go all the way back to Jesus' parting promise to his followers that "I am with you always until the end of the age" (Matt 28:20). Christians have relied on that promise for the past two millennia, believing that Jesus would never abandon the Church. We celebrate the feast of Pentecost as a commemoration of Jesus offering his Spirit to the Church to guide and direct the community of faith across the centuries. It is the Holy Spirit whom we believe works to keep the Church faithful to the Gospel. This fundamental conviction of Catholicism, that through the power of the Spirit Christ will not abandon his Church, is often referred to as the indefectibility of the Church.

Long before Christians began using such technical terms as "infallibility," there was an ancient conviction that the Holy Spirit did indeed protect the Church from error. Early church writers like St. Irenaeus of Lyon, St. Augustine, St. Vincent of Lérins and others held that when all the churches were in agreement on a matter of faith, that teaching could be viewed as completely trustworthy by believers. This ancient intuition reflects the broadest and most inclusive understanding of infallibility, namely the belief that infallibility is given to the whole Church in order to keep the Church faithful to the Gospel. The Second Vatican Council articulated this belief quite clearly when it wrote: "The whole body of the faithful who have received an anointing which comes from the holy one cannot be mistaken in belief" (LG, #12).

The early Church also recognized that while the Holy Spirit animated the whole Church, the bishops were given a particular gift, "a charism of truth," that would enable them to faithfully proclaim the apostolic faith. By the end of the first millennium, it was commonly held that when all the bishops gathered in an ecumenical council to teach on faith and morals, and their teaching was received by all the churches, that teaching was protected from error and normative for belief. The infallibility given to the whole Church was, in a distinctive way, exercised by the college of bishops, especially when they were gathered in an ecumenical council and were intent on definitively pronouncing on a matter revealed by God.

From the beginning of the second century, there was also a common conviction that the church of Rome held a special position of privilege among the communion of churches. As centuries went by, the prestige given to the church of Rome was extended more and more to the bishop of Rome. During that time history showed that on a number of disputed questions (e.g., when the feast of Easter should be celebrated or whether to re-baptize apostates who returned to the Church) Rome was consistently on the side that "won the day." Many looked to Rome as a particularly reliable witness to the Good News of Jesus Christ. By the end of the first millennium, the growing recognition that Rome *had not erred* led to the conviction that Rome *could not err*. The belief that the pope could teach with the charism of infallibility would soon be commonly accepted in the Church even as there were disagreements regarding the scope and conditions for exercising papal infallibility. Finally, at the First Vatican Council, the bishops solemnly defined what is called the dogma of papal infallibility. At the Second Vatican Council this teaching on the infallibility of the papacy was reaffirmed.

According to Vatican II's Dogmatic Constitution on the Church, *Lumen gentium,* there are three ways in which the Church's teaching office can exercise the gift of infallibility, as indicated in the chart appearing earlier in this chapter. The first two are exercises of what is often called the *extraordinary magisterium,* because it is only exercised relatively rarely and in "extraordinary" circumstances. We will consider the third way in the next section of this chapter.

First, all the bishops together (including, always, the bishop of Rome) can solemnly define a dogma when they are gathered at an ecumenical council. This has usually occurred when the bishops recognized that there was a serious attack on the faith of the Church. So, for example, the Council of Nicaea solemnly defined that the Word, the second person of the Trinity, was "one in being" *(homoousios)* with God the Father. Many of our most basic Christian convictions about Christ and the Trinity were solemnly defined by ecumenical councils in the first millennium. This does not mean, of course, that *every* teaching of an ecumenical council is an exercise of infallibility. The Second Vatican Council, for example, did not invoke the charism of infallibility in its own teaching.

At Vatican I the council explicitly announced its intention to issue a solemn definition with the following formulation, "we teach and define as a divinely revealed dogma . . . ."[3] However, when considering councils before the modern period, when these distinctions were not as well established, it is more difficult to know when a council intended to solemnly define a teaching. Scholars must carefully study the wording of conciliar decrees and consider the council *acta* (formal records of council debates) in order to determine the intentions of a council.

Second, the bishop of Rome, in communion with his fellow bishops, can also solemnly define a dogma of the Church. This was first explicitly taught at Vatican I. But the council specified a number of important limits and conditions for the exercise of papal infallibility. The council taught that the pope could only teach infallibly, *ex cathedra*, that is "from the chair of Peter," as universal pastor of the whole Church. In the past there have been popes who have written theological or historical works. Even though they were popes, they were writing as theologians or historians. In these instances, the council agreed, the pope did not exercise the charism of infallibility.[4] A pope could only teach infallibly when he officially taught as the universal pastor of the whole Church.

The council also insisted that popes could not define "new doctrine" but only that which had been divinely revealed and belonged to the apostolic faith. Consequently, according to Catholic teaching, the pope cannot exercise the gift of infallibility in teaching on any matter he wishes—he cannot solemnly define, for example, that the University of Notre Dame (my alma mater) is the best Catholic college in the world, true though it might be! The pope cannot teach infallibly on matters of politics or science but only on that which directly concerns "faith and morals."

Finally, the council taught that the solemn definitions of popes were "irreformable" of themselves and did not require the consent of the Church. This clause is often misunderstood and can give the impression that the pope can act as a kind of church "lone ranger" apart from the other bishops. This was not the intent of Vatican I. For several centuries a viewpoint had been lurking around in the Church that held that, when the pope defines something, it cannot be considered binding until after the bishops had officially ratified the teaching. Vatican I rejected this position, not because they viewed the pope as someone who could or would act independent of the other bishops but because they assumed that a pope would always be in relationship with his other bishops, communicating with them and seeking their counsel. All the council was saying was that it was not necessary to impose a *juridical* ratification by the other bishops. It is surely significant that before Pope Pius IX solemnly defined the dogma of the Immaculate Conception (1854), and before Pope Pius XII solemnly defined the Assumption of Mary (1950), both popes made a point of first writing to all of the bishops and inquiring after the belief of the Church on these matters.

Actual exercises of papal infallibility have been relatively rare in the history of the Church. Though lists of papal definitions differ somewhat (before the modern age, popes, like councils, did not explicitly announce when they were exercising the charism of infallibility, therefore, determining instances of the exercise of papal infallibility requires careful historical research), one scholar, Francis Sullivan, lists five instances in which popes have solemnly defined a dogma, independent of an ecumenical council:[5] (1) Benedict XII's teaching on the beatific vision in *Benedictus Deus* [1336]; (2) Innocent X's condemnation of five Jansenist propositions in *Cum occasione* [1653]; (3) Pius VI's condemnation of seven Jansenist propositions articulated at the Synod of Pistoia in *Auctorem fidei* [1794]; (4) Pius IX's definition of the Immaculate Conception in *Ineffabilis Deus* [1854]; (5) Pius XII's definition of the Assumption of Mary in *Munificentissimus Deus* [1950].

THE ORDINARY UNIVERSAL MAGISTERIUM

As we have seen, the two most commonly known ways of exercising infallibility in church teaching are instances of the extraordinary magisterium and are concerned with the solemn definitions of ecumenical councils and of popes. However, Catholicism also acknowledges a third engagement of the charism of infallibility in church teaching. In many ways it is the most ancient.

There are many church teachings that have been commonly accepted as divinely revealed even though they have never been solemnly defined by a pope or council. We should remember that popes and councils generally defined dogmas only if these teachings were being seriously challenged. But what about the many church teachings that Christians have viewed as central to their faith but which were never seriously challenged and therefore were never formally defined by a pope or council? We might think of the Church's belief in the communion of saints or in the resurrection of the body. These teachings are central to the Catholic faith even though they have never been solemnly defined.

Catholicism teaches that when such teachings have been taught consistently by all of the bishops in their own dioceses as teachings that must be held as definitive and not simply as a probable opinion or as likely to be true, even though the bishops are not formally defining these teachings, they are exercising the charism of infallibility. This third form of exercising the charism of infallibility is called the *ordinary universal magisterium*.

It is possible for there to be a non-infallible exercise of the ordinary universal magisterium. The best example of this would be the teaching of an ecumenical council when it is not issuing a solemn definition. It would be "ordinary" teaching because there is no solemn definition, and "universal" because it engages the whole college of bishops. Other instances of a non-infallible exercise of the ordinary universal magisterium would be the situation in which the bishops, while dispersed throughout the world, held a common judgment regarding a particular teaching but were *not* agreed that the teaching should be held as definitive.

It is not easy for ordinary Catholics today to recognize the distinct modes in which the pope and bishops exercise their teaching office. Sometimes theologians can help identify when these various forms of magisterial teaching are being engaged. For obvious reasons, the most important distinction concerns whether or not the Church's teaching office intends to exercise the charism of infallibility in a particular teaching act. Canon law provides an important principle in this regard. Canon 749§3 states that "no doctrine is understood to be infallibly defined unless it is clearly established as such." Essentially this means that if there is a question as to whether the magisterium has taught something infallibly, the burden of proof is on the magisterium to demonstrate that it is doing so in accord with the accepted conditions established in church tradition. In the face of doubt regarding the possibility of an infallible teaching act, one should presume that the charism of infallibility has not been engaged until it is clearly demonstrated otherwise.

This chapter has considered the diverse ways in which the pope and bishops can fulfill their teaching office. For Catholics this teaching authority is a gift to the Church, guiding the community of believers on the path of salvation. Of course, there are those who see the very existence of such a teaching office as out of step with the terms of modernity in which all forms of authority are subject to challenge. There are others who, fearful of the dizzying atmosphere of change in which we live, cling to easy certitudes and grant to the magisterium of the Church an inflated authority that ignores important distinctions in the exercise of authoritative church teaching. It is one aim of this book to help Catholics avoid both tendencies.

DISPUTED QUESTIONS

1) When the bishops at Vatican II raised the issue of an episcopal synod, many had in mind the kind of structure common to the Eastern Churches, that is, a permanent or standing synod of bishops with deliberative authority that would assist the pope in the governance of the Church. The offices of the Roman Curia (e.g., the Congregation for the Doctrine of the Faith) would then be responsible to this standing synod. Many critics believe that the synods that emerged out of Pope Paul VI's *Apostolica sollicitudo* (1965) fell short of this vision. These synods have only a consultative role, meet for a short period of time every few years, have little control over the agenda, and cede to the pope responsibility for issuing a public report on their proceedings. Many bishops at the council saw the synod as a way of restoring the authority of the bishops and placing the Roman Curia in service of the bishops' unique ministry, yet the current structure still gives the Roman Curia *de facto* authority over the bishops.

2) *Apostolos suos* has not ended debate on the authority of episcopal conferences. Read carefully, the document gives the

impression that the authority of episcopal conferences is nothing more than either the aggregate authority of the individual bishops (when the bishops unanimously approve a document) or the authority of papal teaching (when the Holy See gives a document its *recognitio*). It becomes difficult, from this perspective, to see any genuine collegial authority in such documents. Some canonists would argue, however, that this concern grants too much authority to a *recognitio*. In canon law, when the Vatican grants a *recognitio* to a document it is not giving that document some new papal authority that it did not already possess but is merely confirming that the contents of the document are in accord with the teaching and law of the universal Church.

Even if *Apostolos suos* restricted the doctrinal teaching authority of episcopal conferences, these conferences continue to play an important role in the life of the Church. For some critics, the expansive role of episcopal conferences continues to be a problem. These critics fear that the enhanced role of episcopal conferences may bring about a return to the kind of church nationalism that appeared in times past under the guise of Gallicanism and Febronianism. They warn of what they see as the bureaucratization of the ministry of the bishop in which individual bishops become little more than functionaries who hide behind episcopal committees and vague declarations that inevitably lose their prophetic bite in the process of achieving episcopal consensus.

3) Over the span of two millennia, the papacy moved from being a court of final appeal that only rarely pronounced on doctrinal matters to a situation today in which the pope is viewed as the chief theologian of the Catholic Church. Some would say that this is an altogether necessary and appropriate development required by the complex demands of a global Church in the modern world. They would point out that the pope stands today as a unique moral voice that speaks with unparalleled spiritual authority. Others worry that the practice of popes writing frequent encyclicals that offer in-depth theological explorations of doctrinal questions makes it difficult to distinguish between normative doctrinal pronouncements and papal theological reflection with which theologians might legitimately differ. They

also wonder whether a strong papal teaching authority risks obscuring the teaching role of the bishops who are often better situated to address questions of local or regional import.

4) One of the difficulties with the exercise of the ordinary universal magisterium lies in the problem of verifying when, in fact, the bishops do share a common judgment that a matter is to be held as definitive. Some theologians have suggested that the teachings proposed infallibly by the ordinary universal magisterium have been teachings that have long been accepted in the Church without controversy. However, in the last thirty years, appeals to this mode of church teaching have been made with regard to more controversial matters. For example, the Congregation for the Doctrine of the Faith has declared that the pope's apostolic letter on the prohibition of women from ordination to the priesthood, *Ordinatio sacerdotalis,* was an example of a papal confirmation of the ordinary universal magisterium. The sense seems to be that where it is difficult to verify whether or not the bishops *are* of one judgment that a matter is to be held as definitive (e.g., the teaching on women's ordination), the pope can resolve that ambiguity through a papal confirmation. But this creates the odd situation in which a pope is exercising his ordinary papal magisterium (which does not engage the charism of infallibility) to confirm that the bishops have taught a particular matter in their ordinary universal magisterium (which does engage the charism of infallibility). The question of how to properly verify the exercise of the ordinary universal magisterium remains hotly debated.

FOR FURTHER READING

Boyle, John P. *Church Teaching Authority: Historical and Theological Studies.* Notre Dame, Ind.: University of Notre Dame Press, 1995.
Gaillardetz, Richard R. "The Ordinary Universal Magisterium: Unresolved Questions." *Theological Studies* 63 (September, 2002) 447–71.
_____. Chapters 6 and 7 of *Teaching with Authority: A Theology of the Magisterium in the Church,* 159–224. Collegeville: The Liturgical Press, 1997.

_____. *Witnesses to the Faith: Community, Infallibility and the Ordinary Magisterium of Bishops.* New York: Paulist, 1992.

Huels, John M. "A Theory of Juridical Documents Based on Canons 29–34." *Studia canonica* 32 (1998) 337–70.

John Paul II, Pope. *Apostolos suos. Origins* 28 (July 30, 1998) 152–58.

Morrisey, Francis G. *Papal and Curial Pronouncements: Their Canonical Significance in Light of the Code of Canon Law.* 2nd edition, revised and updated by Michel Thériault. Ottawa: Faculty of Canon Law, St. Paul University, 1995.

Örsy, Ladislas. *The Church: Learning and Teaching.* Wilmington, Del.: Glazier, 1987.

Sullivan, Francis A. *Creative Fidelity: Weighing and Interpreting Documents of the Magisterium.* New York: Paulist, 1996.

_____. *Magisterium: Teaching Office in the Catholic Church.* New York: Paulist, 1983.

_____. "The Teaching Authority of Episcopal Conferences." *Theological Studies* 63 (September, 2002) 472–93.

Tillard, Jean-Marie. *Bishop of Rome.* Wilmington, Del.: Glazier, 1983.

Welch, Lawrence J. "The Infallibility of the Ordinary Universal Magisterium: A Critique of Some Recent Observations." *Heythrop Journal* 39 (1998) 18–36.

SIX

WHAT IS DOGMA
AND DOCTRINE?

Ask a Catholic how many sacraments there are and the answer is simple: seven. How many commandments are there? Ten. A little research reveals that in the history of the Church there have been twenty-one ecumenical or general councils and 262 popes (with a few of each in dispute). The revised Code of Canon Law contains 1752 canons. So why is it that if you ask a Catholic how many dogmas there are in Catholic teaching they cannot give an answer? They can tell you how many articles there are in the creed, but the creeds do not offer exhaustive lists of dogma. They can tell you how many paragraphs there are in the catechism, but then not every catechism paragraph constitutes a distinct Catholic dogma either.

The reason for this curiosity lies in the theology of revelation. A propositional view of revelation regards revelation as nothing more than a collection of individual truths or propositional statements. Those who hold such a view of revelation must surely expect to find a finite number of church teachings, if only they look hard enough. But Vatican II taught that revelation cannot be reduced to a collection of statements or discrete truths. Revelation is disclosed, ultimately, not in a statement or a text but in a person, Jesus Christ. Christ is the fullness of divine revelation, he is "both the mediator and the sum total of revelation" (DV #2).

All church dogma and doctrine are the fruit of the Church's communal meditation on the one revelation of God in Christ. For example, the internal unity of the creed is reflected in the diverse ways in which the creeds have been divided. The Apostle's Creed, by tradition, consists of twelve articles. Yet it is also possible to divide it, along with the

90

Nicene-Constantinopolitan Creed, into three articles, each dedicated to a person of the Trinity. Alternatively, one might read the entire creed as the articulation of the one triune mystery of God's saving love made effective through the Word and in the Spirit.

What the creeds testify to above all is the unity of the one divine revelation. A simple analogy may help. Imagine a powerful lamp projecting a single beam of light on a blank wall. What we see is one beam of light. We might think of this light as the unity of the one revelation of God. This one revelation has been communicated into human history from the beginning of time through the divine Word and made effective by the power of the Spirit. In "the fullness of time," Christians believe that this one revelation was expressed in an unsurpassable manner in Jesus of Nazareth. Inasmuch as we reflect on this revelation in terms of its source, the triune God, we will focus on the unity of God's perfect self-communication.

Let us return to the image of the one beam of light. What happens if we place a prism in front of that beam? What we will see projected on the wall is not an undifferentiated beam but a plurality of colors spread across a spectrum. The prism might be thought of as human history. The unity of God's revelation is refracted into a diversity of mediations in human history. As humans, our only access to the unity of the beam of light, the one revelation of God, is through the historical diversity of its manifestations.

Christianity asserts that we have encountered the one revelation of God in the covenants recounted by the ancient ancestors of Israel, in the prophets and in the various ways in which Israel preserved their encounters with their God in their sacred writings. Christianity has encountered God's revelation in the oral and then written testimony of the early Christians who first walked with Jesus on the shores of the Sea of Galilee and then encountered him as risen. That revelation continues to be handed on and received in the liturgy, in the teachings of councils and popes, in the theological meditations of great Christian theologians (often called "doctors of the Church"), in the dramatic testimony of saints and martyrs, and in the more mundane testimony of simple believers struggling to follow the Gospel in their daily lives. In other words, if we shift our attention from the source of divine revelation, to our experience of it, we move from unity to plurality.

This is why we do not number dogmas. Catholics believe that dogmas are but specific historical mediations of the one revelation of God.

When we forget that, when we treat dogmas as if they were revelation it-self, instead of *mediations* of God's revelation, we flirt with a kind of fundamentalism. This Catholic fundamentalism is every bit as dangerous as biblical fundamentalism; in both instances a written text or statement is viewed as revelation itself rather than an inspired or Spirit-assisted testimony, manifestation or mediation of God's saving reality.

Humans live in history and, consequently, our encounter with God will always be mediated through historical expressions, be it the Bible or a particular ritual act or dogmatic statement. In Catholicism, church teaching remains important, not as an end in itself, but because of the way in which it can direct our gaze toward God, illuminating for us the ever incomprehensible mystery of God.

THE FUNCTIONS OF CHURCH TEACHING

The words "dogma" and "doctrine" are often used interchangeably. For the sake of greater precision, however, we will need to distinguish these two terms. In Scripture and early church usage, the term "dogma" carried a wide range of meanings. However, beginning in the eighteenth century, "dogma" came to refer to those propositional formulations thought to be divinely revealed. This understanding of dogma has continued up to the present.

> *A dogma is any propositional formulation which is (1) divinely revealed and (2) proposed as such by the magisterium, either through a solemn definition of a pope or council, or by the teaching of the college of bishops in their ordinary and universal magisterium.*

Although the term "doctrine" is sometimes used as a synonym for dogma, its field of meaning is much broader.

> *A doctrine is any authoritative or normative formulation of a belief of the Church, whether revealed or not. A church doctrine is intended to articulate a formal belief of the Church that it draws in some fashion from its reflection on divine revelation even if it may not itself be divinely revealed.*

All dogmas are doctrines, not all doctrines are dogmas.

The earliest instances of church dogma or doctrine of any kind was found in the ancient creeds produced by the early Church. These creeds were initially developed for use in sacramental initiation and worship. We tend to miss this because of changes in the way we understand the verb "to believe." The Greek verb *pisteuo,* like the Latin *credo,* originally had a performative, promise-making sense (literally "to faith . . ."). To say "I believe in God" was less reporting a matter of fact than it was a personal commitment to a relationship with this God. The profession of faith had the character of a pledge or commitment, not unlike the pledge that spouses make to one another in their wedding vows. This has important implications for those involved in catechetical ministry. It suggests that the creeds be used, particularly in catechumenal ministry, as an invitation to enter into the Catholic Christian community's life of faith and worship and not primarily as orthodoxy checklists.

Over time, the creedal statements of the Church began to play a more "regulative" role. They became normative expressions of "right belief" in the Christian faith. These statements usually emerged at points in the history of the Church when fundamental tenets of the Church's faith were being threatened. Their formulation was determined by the controversy to which they were responding. For that reason, dogmatic statements cannot be treated as exhaustive, comprehensive presentations of the faith of the Church. Rather, when properly interpreted within their historical, cultural, linguistic, philosophical and theological contexts, they offer sure guideposts which articulate authentic conceptual expressions of the living tradition of the Church.

Official church teachings are not intended to be parroted in theological and catechetical discourse. Such teachings ought to function as fixed reference points for theological discussion and catechetical ministry. Any *alternative* theological formulations must be congruent, that is, intellectually reconcilable, with the appropriate doctrinal teaching. Indeed, it would be a grave pastoral error to rely exclusively or even primarily on doctrinal statements in preaching and catechetical ministry. The somewhat dry and precise conceptual language of doctrinal statements rarely elicits conversion and growth in faith. These interior movements are usually encouraged by narrative and more symbolic, poetic forms of expression. Far more have been converted to discipleship in Christ by an experience of the liturgy, the moving testimony of the saints of the Church, the witness of the ordinary heroism of a fellow believer, or the

[handwritten margin notes: doctrine not the means to draw people in to the Church]

poetic oratory of a spirit-filled preacher than by any conciliar decree or catechism summary statement.

GRADATIONS IN CHURCH TEACHING

Over the course of almost two thousand years, the Christian community has found it necessary to make formal doctrinal pronouncements against perceived threats to the integrity of the faith. Some of these pronouncements helped clarify fundamental church tenets. Others dealt with fairly specific issues that later generations would view as peripheral. The mature Christian must be able to distinguish between teachings expressive of those vital faith commitments that constitute the core of our Christian identity, and those which play a more dependent role. There has gradually emerged within the Roman Catholic communion a set of distinctions regarding church teaching that can help us in making these determinations.

GRADATIONS OF CHURCH TEACHING

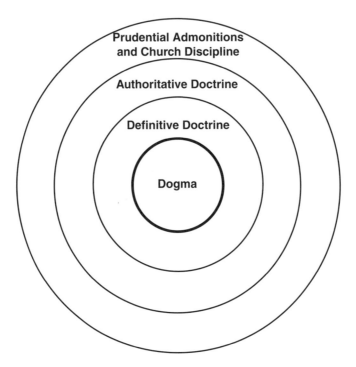

Dogma

Most important is that privileged set of teachings that we call *dogma*. These teachings communicate God's saving message as revealed to us in Scripture and tradition. Some of these are relatively technical, pronounced in general councils or papal decrees to address issues which may not concern us today. However, most of the more significant dogmatic teachings are found in the basic creedal statements of the Church like the Nicene-Constantinopolitan Creed which we profess in the Sunday liturgy. They concern such central aspects of our faith as the divinity of Christ and the bodily resurrection. These teachings, because they are proposed with the charism of infallibility, are held to be irreversible in character. These terms have often occasioned misunderstanding so it will be worthwhile to consider them in more detail.

The Charism of Infallibility and the Irreversibility of Certain Church Teachings

To say that a dogma is irreversible (some church documents prefer the term "irreformable" or "definitive") means that this teaching is not erroneous—that, adequately interpreted, it will not lead believers away from the path of salvation. At the same time, it is still a human expression that, in its formulation, can always be improved upon. Every dogmatic teaching necessarily makes use of certain cultural, philosophical, theological and linguistic constructs, all of which are human inventions. Thus although Catholic Christians believe that an irreversible teaching is a reliable mediation of divine revelation that will never be "wrong," it will always be possible to adopt new and more adequate philosophical, theological and linguistic constructs aimed at a faithful articulation of revelation.

Irreversible dogmas are taught by the magisterium and believed by the whole people of God with the charism of infallibility. Technically speaking, infallibility refers to a charism that assists the Church as a whole in a *judgment* of belief and the teaching office of the Church in a teaching *judgment.* The object of the exercise of the charism of infallibility is a teaching deemed to be irreversible (irreformable or definitive).

The gift of infallibility is not some magic wand that popes and bishops get to wield; it is not simply one of the "perks" that come with the job. Infallibility is God's promise to the Church that *when it comes to matters pertaining to our salvation* we can be confident that church teaching will be a sure guide. This does not mean that the Church cannot commit error at all. The pope and bishops guide us in Christian living at many levels. For over two thousand years church teaching has been remarkably trustworthy and Catholic Christians have justifiably given to church teaching the presumption of truth. Nevertheless, the Catholic Church recognizes that some of its teaching is not necessarily divinely revealed, and that in those instances there is the remote possibility of church error. We have had popes and bishops who have led immoral lives and done many imprudent things. We have also had popes and bishops who have offered non-revealed teachings that later were seen to be inadequate if not simply wrong (e.g., the Church's condemnation of usury or its official tolerance of the institution of slavery). What the doctrine of infallibility promises us is that the Church will never be in error *in matters pertaining to our salvation.*

To understand better how infallibility functions in the life of the Church, let me suggest a second analogy regarding "light." The first analogy demonstrated how revelation comes to humankind through the prism of human history. Now we will consider how a revealed dogma functions in illuminating, through an act of faith, the mystery of God revealed in Christ by the power of the Holy Spirit. The analogy is different because we are now considering, not how revelation comes to us, but how, in the act of Christian faith, church dogmas can return our gaze toward God, drawing us into the life of communion.

Imagine that a local parish has contracted a world renowned artist to create a sculpture of Christ, the Good Shepherd. After a long wait the statue finally is to be unveiled in front of the church. Parishioners are invited to drive by in the evening to see it beautifully illuminated by a specially designed set of floodlights. I am sure that the pastor (and the artist!) would be quite dismayed if parishioners driving by were to exclaim: "My, what gorgeous floodlights!" The point of the floodlights is not to draw attention to themselves but to illuminate the beautiful statue.

So it is with church dogma. They are like floodlights insofar as their function lies not in drawing our attention to them in their own right, but in their ability to direct our gaze toward Christ who is himself the indescribable beauty of God and our one true salvation. As with all analogies, there are limits to its applicability. For God is not an object to be observed but a divine Subject encountered in faith as incomprehensible Mystery. Yet dogmas do illuminate for us, however imperfectly, something true and indispensable about the holy mystery of God. With that in mind, let us return to the statue and floodlights.

When the floodlights are properly aligned, we don't notice them at all but rather gaze upon the work of art. But what if the floodlights were misaligned and drew our gaze, not to the sculpture, but to the church's rain gutter? For us to encounter the artist's work, we have to trust that the lights will be properly aligned. When it comes to church dogma, we must also trust that they are properly aligned, that they are indeed illuminating Christ and the way of salvation. We rely on the certain knowledge that they will not misdirect our gaze like poorly aligned floodlights. This is the purpose of the charism of infallibility; it gives us the confidence that our gaze is not being misdirected. Church dogma does indeed faithfully and without error mediate divine revelation and illuminate faithfully, if imperfectly, the incomprehensible mystery of God.

There is another insight to be drawn from our analogy. If we drive by the church at night and the floodlights are properly aligned, they allow us to gaze upon the sculpture. However, it is still possible to improve the floodlights. The artist might ask that more powerful lamps be employed to better illuminate his work. The floodlights, as they are, still function correctly and direct the viewers' gaze to the sculpture but they can be improved upon. So too the exercise of infallibility promises us that a dogma will not misdirect our gaze; it will faithfully mediate God's self-gift. But the Catholic Church also recognizes that it is still possible to re-formulate our dogmatic definitions. Further study and theological reflection can improve and refine the way we articulate church teaching. To say that a dogma has been taught infallibly means that we can trust that it will not lead us away from the path of salvation; it does not preclude our finding better ways to communicate its abiding truth.

Most of the significant dogmatic teachings of the Church are found in the creeds that we recite in the liturgy. Beyond these there are other dogmatic teachings, proposed by popes or councils, generally in response to some controversy. Examples of church dogma would include the belief in the divinity of Christ, the law of love, the resurrection of the body, and the affirmation of the real presence of Christ in the Eucharist. All such teachings do, according to Catholic teaching, faithfully mediate some aspect of divine revelation. This does not mean, however, that every dogma is equally central to the life of the Church.

The Hierarchy of Truths

The Second Vatican Council recognized a certain ordering of church dogma in its teaching on the "hierarchy of truths." The Decree on

Ecumenism, *Unitatis redintegratio,* offered guidelines for how
Catholic theologians ought to conduct themselves in formal ecumenical dialogue with other non-Catholic Christians. It then offered this
counsel:

> When comparing doctrines with one another, they should remember
> that in catholic doctrine there exists an order or "hierarchy" of truths,
> since they vary in their relation to the foundation of the christian faith
> (UR #11).

The conciliar text insists that church dogmas must be understood and
interpreted in the light of their relationship to the foundation of Christian faith. This "foundation" refers to the entire economy of salvation—
what God has done for us in Christ by the power of the Spirit. The
council taught that church dogmas have differing relations or links to
this foundation. This interpretation is confirmed by the 1973 CDF
declaration "In Defense of Catholic Doctrine," article 4, which affirms that some dogmas or "truths" lean on more principal "truths"
and are illumined by them. It is also true that some dogmatic pronouncements addressed questions that were quite important during
one period of church history, but have diminished in their importance
today. This insight can be helpful for catechists who are sometimes
tempted to treat every dogmatic teaching as equally weighty.

Let me offer an example. One of the issues with which Christians
struggled during the fifth through the seventh centuries was how to
hold together both the belief that Jesus was the incarnation of the second person of the Trinity and the conviction that Jesus possessed two
natures, one human and the other divine. Some theological approaches
so emphasized the two distinct natures of Christ that it often seemed
that Christ had developed a kind of "split personality." Others so emphasized the unity of Christ as the incarnation of the Word, that his
distinctive humanity was undervalued. Those who chose to emphasize
the "oneness of Christ" over against his possessing a distinct human
nature were called "Monophysites." In the seventh century, as part of
an effort to bring the Monophysites back into the Church, some theologians offered a compromise theory that affirmed that Christ possessed two distinct natures but had but one "will." This theory came
to be known as "monothelitism," and it was ultimately condemned at
the Third Council of Constantinople, which declared that Christ possessed "two wills." In the context of the debates that raged at the time

regarding the integrity of Christ's full humanity, this was an important declaration. However, in later periods of the Church, the question of whether Christ possessed one or two wills became less significant. Today, if you filled a room with educated Catholics (ordained and lay) and asked them whether Christ possesses one will or two, you might encounter confusion and disagreement. This would mean nothing regarding the orthodoxy of one group or another; all it would prove is that this way of formulating ancient Christological teaching no longer has purchase on modern Catholics. It is not that Constantinople III was wrong; it is just that its Christological formulation is no longer central to the faith consciousness of Catholics today.

Definitive Doctrine

There is a tendency among some today to artificially elevate all church teaching to the status of dogma. Yet in fact there are three other categories of church teaching that are not dogmatic, properly speaking. These include a second category of church teaching referred to as *definitive doctrine.* This category has only recently been explored in any detail by bishops and theologians. It includes teachings that are not divinely revealed but are *necessary for safeguarding and expounding divine revelation.* Because it is assumed that these teachings are necessary for preserving divine revelation, these teachings, like dogmas, are also taught with the charism of infallibility and, as such, are also irreversible (irreformable). One example of a teaching often placed in this category is the Council of Trent's determination of the books included in the canon of the Bible.

Authoritative Doctrine

In addition to *dogma and definitive doctrine,* a third category of church teaching is *authoritative doctrine.* These are teachings that the magisterium proposes authoritatively to guide the faith of believers. Authoritative doctrine is drawn from the wisdom of the Church as it reflects on Scripture and tradition. Included among *authoritative doctrine* are many concrete moral teachings such as the immorality of directly targeting civilians in an act of war or the prohibition of certain reproductive technologies like *in vitro* fertilization. Yet even as these teachings are proposed authoritatively, the Church's teaching office is not ready to commit itself irrevocably to them. Practically speaking, this means that, however remote, there is a possibility of error with respect to these teachings.

Many people believe that acknowledging the possibility of error in church teaching will undermine the authority of the magisterium. If one admits the possibility of error, they fear, believers would lose confidence in the Church's teaching authority. I am inclined to believe that quite the opposite is the case. It is a mistake to think that unless the Church's teaching office is infallible, it cannot possess any real authority.

Consider the way in which we view authority in other spheres of our lives. When I go to a doctor because I am experiencing chest pains, I recognize that there is a remote possibility that the doctor will misdiagnose my condition. I still grant the doctor authority even though I know that her authority is not infallible. I trust that this doctor has been properly trained and certified and shown herself to be a reliable physician. My recognition of the remote possibility of error is not an impediment to acknowledging her authority. In the same way, the Catholic Church teaches that it is protected from error when it pronounces on God's self-gift in revelation. In other instances it may teach with authority, but that authority does not exclude the possibility of error.

An honest acknowledgment that the magisterium is not always immune from error would, I believe, actually enhance the credibility of the Church's teaching office. Many Catholics today know enough about past church teachings, like its condemnation of usury, to have already accepted the fact that the magisterium has erred in the past. When church leaders appear reluctant to acknowledge both past errors and the possibility of future ones, they risk undermining the credibility of the magisterium altogether. An honest and forthright acknowledgement of the limits of authority, accompanied by a judicious restraint regarding the frequency with which that authority is exercised, would give subsequent authoritative pronouncements greater weight.

Concrete Applications of Church Teaching, Prudential Admonitions and Church Discipline

Finally, a fourth category of church teaching would include any of a variety of teachings that, technically, would fall short of formal, authoritative doctrine. A good example is found in Catholic moral teaching. The American bishops in their pastoral letter *The Challenge of*

Peace distinguished between binding moral principles and concrete moral applications about which Catholics could disagree in good faith. For example, the American bishops' condemnation of first use of nuclear weapons constituted a quite concrete application of specific moral principles in a particular context. The bishops held that prudential judgments of this kind, regarding the concrete application of church teaching, must be given "serious attention and consideration by Catholics as they determine whether their moral judgments are consistent with the Gospel."[1] Nevertheless, they admitted that Catholics might legitimately differ with the bishops regarding these moral applications and prudential judgments.

Also included in this fourth category would be prudential admonitions about questionable aspects of certain theological writings or particular instances of church discipline. For example, the requirement of celibacy for diocesan priests is a matter of church discipline, not church doctrine.

This set of gradations in church teaching cannot, of course, do justice to the richness and multi-textured character of the Catholic doctrinal tradition. It will not always be easy to determine the precise authoritative status of one or another particular teaching. It remains, in no small part, for the theological and catechetical community to assist the whole people of God in the important ecclesial discernment necessary if Catholics are to grasp the proper demands set before them by the teaching of the Church.

DISPUTED QUESTIONS

1) In ecumenical theology, the Second Vatican Council's teaching on the hierarchy of truths has a particular significance. Many theologians contend that the Church has yet to fully exploit this important insight that not every dogmatic teaching in the Catholic church is equally central to "the foundations of the Christian faith." For example, some scholars have suggested that it need not be necessary to require as a condition for ecumenical reunion that non-Catholic Christian communions assent to *every* dogmatic teaching proposed infallibly within the Catholic tradition. These scholars contend that there are certain dogmatic teachings, such as those related to Mary, that

while divinely revealed, simply confirm more basic truths shared by all Christians (e.g., the universality of redemption and the resurrection of the body).

2) An important disputed question concerns the authoritative status of church moral teaching. It is commonly accepted that some moral teachings of the Church do have dogmatic status, such as the law of love and the affirmation of the inalienable dignity of the human person. But what about more specific moral teachings like the Church's prohibition of artificial birth control or its just-war teaching? Few theologians believe that teachings of this sort have been taught infallibly, but the more difficult question concerns whether they *could* be taught infallibly. In other words, does the scope of infallibility extend to more specific moral questions? Those who answer in the affirmative highlight the integrity of divine revelation and the way in which more specific moral teachings, even if they are not technically divinely revealed, are so closely related to divine revelation that they could also be taught infallibly. Other theologians argue that specific moral teachings like the prohibition of artificial birth control depend too much on empirical data subject to change (e.g., embryological studies of what transpires in the earliest stages of conception) to be able to be taught infallibly. Of course, they would insist, these teachings would still possess a normative status as authoritative doctrine.

3) Many questions have been raised regarding the second category of church teaching, referred to as "definitive doctrine." The assertion that such teachings are protected by the charism of infallibility has been commonly assumed, both at Vatican I and Vatican II. However this assertion has never itself been taught infallibly.

There are also significant disagreements regarding the scope of definitive doctrine. Pope John Paul II, in the papal document *Ad tuendam fidem,* mandated an addition to the Code of Canon Law concerning definitive doctrine. That addition states that definitive doctrines are teachings "*required* for the sacred preservation and faithful explanation of the same deposit of faith . . ." (c. 750.2). Other, less authoritative, documents broaden the scope of definitive doctrine considerably to include teachings that are "connected" to divine revelation by "logical or historical necessity." Some theologians have voiced their concern that this broader definition of the scope of definitive doctrine is sufficiently malleable as to allow any church teaching to be included in this category.

The Congregation for the Doctrine of the Faith has determined that the Church's teaching on the prohibition of the ordination of women to the priesthood is an infallibly proposed definitive doctrine. This conclusion has drawn considerable attention to this relatively new category of church teaching as some scholars have found the arguments put forward by the CDF unconvincing.

FOR FURTHER READING

Congregation for the Doctrine of the Faith, "In Defense of Catholic Doctrine" [*Mysterium Ecclesiae*]. *Origins* 3 (July 19, 1973) 97–112.

Dulles, Avery. *The Craft of Theology: From Symbol to System.* New York: Crossroad, 1992.

_____. *Models of Revelation.* Garden City: Doubleday, 1983.

_____. *Revelation Theology: A History.* New York: Crossroad, 1969.

_____. *The Survival of Dogma.* New York: Crossroad, 1982.

Gaillardetz, Richard R. "*Ad tuendam fidem*: An Emerging Pattern in Current Papal Teaching." *New Theology Review* 12 (February, 1999) 43–51.

_____. Chapter 4 in *Teaching with Authority: A Theology of the Magisterium in the Church,* 101–28. Collegeville: The Liturgical Press, 1997.

Haight, Roger. *Dynamics of Theology.* New York: Paulist, 1990.

Hines, Mary. *The Transformation of Dogma: An Introduction to Karl Rahner on Doctrine.* New York: Paulist, 1989.

International Theological Commission, "On the Interpretation of Dogmas." *Origins* 20 (May 17, 1990) 1–14.

John Paul II, Pope. *Ad Tuendam Fidem. Origins* 28 (July 16, 1998) 113–16.

Marthaler, Berard. *The Creed: The Apostolic Faith in Contemporary Theology,* rev. ed. Mystic, Conn.: Twenty-Third Publications, 1993.

PART THREE

THE AUTHORITY OF
THE BELIEVING COMMUNITY

SEVEN

WHAT IS THE SENSE
OF THE FAITHFUL?

"The Church is not a democracy!" As I remarked in an earlier chapter, this is a slogan one often hears whenever the possibility of introducing more participatory church structures is raised. The assumption
is that participation of the faithful in the processes of official church
teaching is an inappropriate application of a secular political model to
the life of the Church. However, I will suggest in this chapter that the
Church's official teaching office is *theologically bound* to consult the
faithful in its teaching process, not as a nod to liberal democratic expectations, but because the nature of the Church demands it.

THE TEACHING OF VATICAN II

One of the most important new developments in the council's theological presentation of the Church was the renewed attention it gave
to pneumatology, the theology of the Holy Spirit. For much of the
history of Western ecclesiology, the role of the Holy Spirit had been
eclipsed by a tendency to think of the Church almost exclusively in its
relation to Christ. The Holy Spirit received very little attention. At
Vatican II, however, we find a renewed appreciation that if, in some
sense, Christ laid the foundations for the Church, it was the Spirit
who continues to animate the Church, guiding it along its pilgrim
journey. This is wonderfully expressed in the following passage from
Lumen gentium:

> The Spirit dwells in the church and in the hearts of the faithful, as in a
> temple, prays and bears witness in them that they are his adopted children.

He guides the church in the way of all truth and, uniting it in fellowship and ministry, bestows upon it different hierarchic and charismatic gifts, and in this way directs it and adorns it with his fruits. By the power of the Gospel he rejuvenates the church, constantly renewing it and leading it to perfect union with its spouse (LG #4).

By appealing to the Holy Spirit as the source of all gifts the council was able to reconcile what had often been opposed. For almost four centuries Catholicism had rallied around the authority of church office (e.g., pope and bishops) while classical Protestantism stressed the indispensability of charisms given to all the faithful. In the above passage the council contends, however, that both office and charism find their source in the work of the Holy Spirit. The authority of church office and the Spirited insight of the faithful cannot be put in opposition to one another because they share the same source. The Spirit builds up the life of the Church in many different ways. Even the teaching ministry of the Church, while exercised in a uniquely authoritative way by the ecclesiastical magisterium, also requires the Spirit-assisted insight of all the faithful.

For centuries Catholicism had been inclined to identify the prophetic office of the Church with the pope and bishops. Yet the council also asserted the role of all the faithful in the prophetic ministry of the Church:

> The holy people of God shares also in Christ's prophetic office: it spreads abroad a living witness to him, especially by a life of faith and love and by offering to God a sacrifice of praise, the fruit of lips confessing his name. The whole body of the faithful who have received an anointing which comes from the holy one cannot be mistaken in belief. It shows this characteristic through the entire people's supernatural sense of the faith, when, "from the bishops to the last of the faithful" it manifests a universal consensus in matters of faith and morals. By this sense of the faith, aroused and sustained by the Spirit of truth, the people of God, guided by the sacred magisterium which it faithfully obeys, receives not the word of human beings, but truly the word of God, "the faith once for all delivered to the saints." The people unfailingly adheres to this faith, penetrates it more deeply through right judgment, and applies it more fully in daily life (LG #12).

Each believer, by virtue of baptism, has a supernatural instinct or sense of the faith (*sensus fidei*) that allows each to recognize God's Word and to respond to it. The individual exercise of this instinct is not, of course, infallible. Nevertheless, the council saw this spiritual instinct as vital to building up the faith of the Church.

In addition to the spiritual sense given to each believer at baptism, we can also speak of the sense of the whole faithful *(sensus fidelium)*, namely, that which the whole people of God in fact believe. This is not always easy to determine, and there will be instances when there is, at a given point in time, no consensus in belief among the faithful. This is more likely to be the case when the Church is considering new and emerging issues or older questions being considered in new contexts. When the faithful are united in their belief, manifesting a true consensus, we can speak of a *consensus fidelium*. It is this situation that the council had in mind when it affirmed the infallibility of the whole people of God. But how is this consensus in belief to be determined? The answer to this question requires a fuller consideration of the relationship between the sense of the faithful and the work of the magisterium.

REFLECTING ON THE SENSE OF FAITH GIVEN TO ALL BELIEVERS

The sense or instinct for the faith *(sensus fidei)* given to each believer in baptism, may be understood in two ways.[1] First, it can refer to a capacity of the individual believer to understand God's revelation addressed to them in love. In this regard we might think of the sense of faith as a kind of spiritual sense or sixth sense. It is this capacity that allows a believer, almost intuitively, to sense what is of God and what is not. But the sense of faith might also be thought of, not only as a capacity, but as an actual perception or imaginative grasp of divine revelation.

This might be understood by returning to the analogy of a work of art employed in the last chapter. When we encounter a piece of art like a beautiful sculpture, it has an effect on us; we receive the art from our own particular perspective. Our own life story, our storehouse of life experiences, inclines us to understand the work of art in a particular way. The work of the artist is completed in our viewing (or, regarding other artistic media, our hearing, touching or reading) the work. We bring something of ourselves to the work of art. So, returning to the sculpture of Christ the Good Shepherd discussed in the last chapter, viewers who might gather around to discuss their impressions of the sculpture will have a shared dimension to their experiences—they are viewing the same sculpture—but their interpretations of it will inevitably

differ. For one viewer the artist may have wonderfully captured childhood images nurtured through repeated stories of the shepherd who
leaves the ninety-nine to seek out the one lost sheep. Yet another
viewer will experience a shock in the viewing as they recognize something in the sculpture quite at odds with their childhood image. That
experience of shock may work on this viewer at some deep level as their
religious imagination subtly re-configures itself around this startlingly
new artistic work. Is it too bold to wonder whether the encounter
with this sculpture will re-shape their personal Christology, a Christology that exists at a level far deeper than that of doctrine, a Christology
that abides in one's imaginative construal of Jesus of Nazareth?

Christians encounter God's divine revelation in the context of a
community of faith. We hear the Scriptures preached to us as a community; we celebrate the liturgy as a community; we meditate before
the crucifix on Good Friday as a community. Yet each of us uniquely
encounters that one revelation, and when we give testimony to our
personal encounter with God's revelation, received and interpreted
within the unique stories of our lives, the community is enriched by
our testimony. In our testimony the Church receives the one revelation of God's love, incarnate in Christ by the power of the Spirit, as
something fresh and vital. Consequently, as the Second Vatican Council observed (DV #8), each believer contributes something to the faith
consciousness of the Church, not only through the faithful acceptance
of church doctrine, but by offering their own imaginative construal of
the divine self-gift they have received within the distinctive framework
of their own life story.

THE RELATIONSHIP BETWEEN THE SENSE OF THE FAITHFUL AND THE TEACHING OFFICE OF THE CHURCH

We already saw how, in the Dogmatic Constitution on Divine Revelation, the council credited the development of tradition itself to the
contributions of the spiritual insights of the faithful.

> This comes about through the contemplation and study of believers
> who ponder these things in their hearts. It comes from the intimate
> sense of spiritual realities which they experience. And it comes from the
> preaching of those who, on succeeding to the office of bishop, have re-
> ceived the sure charism of truth (DV #8).

This passage proposes that the testimony of the faithful and the ministry of the bishops share in the "traditioning" process of the Church. The council returns to this conviction in *Lumen gentium* #35 where the bishops write:

> [Christ] fulfils this prophetic office, not only through the hierarchy who teach in his name and by his power but also through the laity. He accordingly both establishes them as witnesses and provides them with an appreciation of the faith *(sensus fidei)* and the grace of the word so that the power of the Gospel may shine out in daily family and social life.

Catholic doctrine teaches unambiguously that the bishops alone possess supreme authority in the Church and, by virtue of their apostolic office, are the authoritative guardians of the faith. But church teaching also holds that the bishops, including the bishop of Rome, do not teach new revelation, but only what has been passed on. How then are we to understand the relationship between the whole people of God who encounter God's revelation in their daily lives and the bishops who must *safeguard* that Word? To explore this further we might consider an image first employed by Cardinal John Henry Newman in the nineteenth century, the *conspiratio fidelium et pastorum*, the "breathing together of the faithful and the pastors."

Newman developed this notion in his famous essay *On Consulting the Faithful in Matters of Doctrine*.[2] In our age it is all too common to see the bishops pitted against the faithful in a relationship of opposition and subordination. Newman's fine image, *conspiratio*, "breathing together," avoids this in two ways. First, we must remember that the pastors are also part of the faithful. A common mistake in popular ecclesiology identifies the faithful with the laity. But as Vatican II taught, the faithful, the *fideles*, are the whole people of God, lay and clergy, so there can be no opposition. The bishop's role of leadership is situated within his common Christian identity as a *Christifidelis*, a "Christian faithful."

Second, Newman's use of the image of "breathing together" reminds us of the Holy Spirit who is the "holy breath" of God. "Breathing together" requires a shared rhythm, if you will, a rhythm established by the Spirit. Newman believed that the one apostolic faith given to the whole Church was manifested in different forms in the life of the Church. To discover this faith one must look to "the mind of the Church."[3] Consequently, in some sense the whole Church could be seen as teachers and learners. Newman broke with the tendency in Catholic thought, at least since the sixteenth century, to divide the Church into two different groups, the teaching church *(ecclesia docens)* and the learning church *(ecclesia discens)*. For Newman the whole Church participated in the handing on of the faith.

This sharing of the roles of teacher and learner was a manifestation of this *conspiratio*. It did not mean for Newman that the bishops abandoned their unique role as authoritative teachers. Rather it meant that before they taught, along with their careful and prayerful study of Scripture and tradition, they might profitably inquire after the insights of the faithful as part of their preparation for teaching. There is evidence that the early Church saw no contradiction in asserting that the bishop was both a teacher and a learner. For example, St. Cyprian wrote:

> But it is unrepentant presumption and insolence that induces men to defend their own perverse errors instead of giving assent to what is right and true, but has come from another. The blessed apostle Paul foresaw this when he wrote to Timothy with the admonition that a bishop should be not wrangling or quarrelsome but gentle and teachable. Now a man is teachable if he is meek and gentle and patient in learning. It is thus a bishop's duty not only to teach but also to learn. For he becomes a better teacher if he makes daily progress and advancement in learning what is better.[4]

This is why Cyprian made such free use of consultation in the exercise of his episcopal office.

In the 1980s the American bishops modeled this kind of consultative process in the way in which they went about producing two seminal pastoral letters, the first on war and peace, and the second on the economy. The promulgation of each of those documents was preceded by extensive listening sessions and open hearings in which the views of experts were considered at great length. Many ecclesiologists consider that procedure to be a model of collaboration between the bishops and the people.

Since the council there has been a good deal of reflection on a concept closely related to the sense of the faithful—the "ecclesial reception" of church teaching. In the early Church the elect who were being prepared to celebrate the Easter sacraments underwent an ancient ritual known as the *traditio-redditio symboli,* "the handing over and giving back of the creed." A copy of the creed would be handed to them, and then they would profess the creed to the community. This ritual action reflects how the faith of the Church is handed on, received and offered anew. The new *General Directory for Catechesis* explains its significance:

> The profession of faith received by the Church *(traditio),* which germi-nates and grows during the catechetical process, is given back *(reddi-tio),* enriched by the values of different cultures. The catechumenate is thus transformed into a center of deepening catholicity and a ferment of ecclesial renewal.[5]

The GDC recognizes that the handing on of the faith is in fact a com-plex reciprocal process in which the elect contribute something posi-tively, in their very act of reception, to the life of the Church. In the act of receiving the faith, the people of God make that faith their own and, in doing so, add something new to the faith.

In the years immediately after the Second Vatican Council, scholars began to pay much more attention to the role of reception in the life of the early Church. They saw ecclesial reception at work in the way in which local churches received (or at times did not receive) the authori-tative pronouncements of synods and councils. For example, it took decades for all the churches to fully "receive" and accept into their life and worship the creeds of the Councils of Nicaea and Constantinople. The process we discussed in Part One by which the churches only gradually accepted the authoritative status of certain biblical texts might also be considered an example of church reception. Reception often oc-curred with respect to the liturgy as when the churches of the West "re-ceived" the Eastern liturgical tradition of the *epiklesis* into their liturgy.

Presupposed in the ecclesial dynamic of "handing on" and "receiv-ing" was a reciprocal relationship between the bishops and their churches. That which was taught by the bishops was always understood, in some sense, to be already in the possession of the Church. Bishops' teaching and ecclesial reception were inseparable elements of the larger process of handing on the apostolic faith.

This ancient process of ecclesial reception was weakened consider-ably over the course of the second millennium. The Church of the late Middle Ages and Counter-Reformation gradually shifted toward a more pyramidal view of the Church built on the foundations of canon law more than theology and the sacraments. During the late Middle Ages the reciprocal relationship of episcopal teaching and ecclesial re-ception gave way to a view of reception governed by the juridical no-tion of obedience.

A JURIDICAL VIEW OF RECEPTION

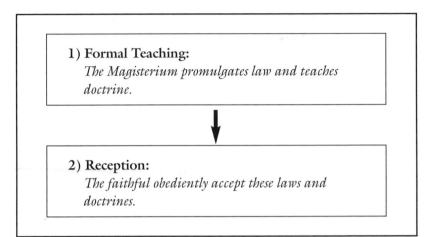

The dynamic understanding of the Christian faith as that which must be proclaimed and received within the life of the Church was replaced by a juridical conception of command-obedience wherein the faithful contributed nothing in the act of obedient reception.

The teaching of Vatican II on the active role of the whole people of God in the Church's "traditioning" process challenged this juridical view without, however, offering a developed alternative. Since the council, theologians have been exploring a model of ecclesial reception more in keeping with the intuitions of the council. Such a model, if it is to be faithful to the council, must affirm that the whole Christian community participates, each in their proper way, in the process of handing on the faith. Yet that model must also acknowledge the unique role of the Church's teaching office. The result would be a view of ecclesial reception reflected in the understanding of the Church as a communion of persons constituted by an interlocking web of mutual and reciprocal relationships. This model will highlight, in particular, the mutual and reciprocal relationships that obtain between the bishops and the whole Christian faithful. The chart below sketches out what such a *communio*-model of reception might look like.

A *COMMUNIO*-MODEL OF RECEPTION

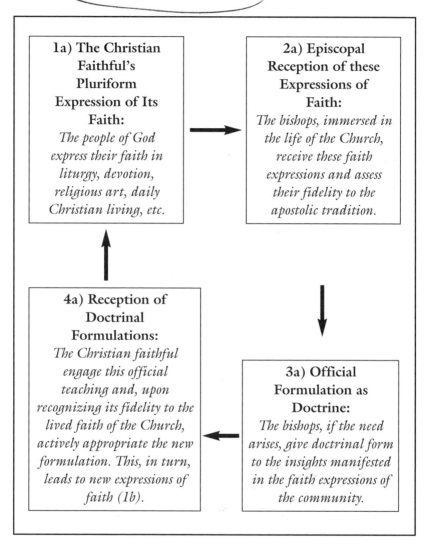

1a) The Christian Faithful's Pluriform Expression of Its Faith:
The people of God express their faith in liturgy, devotion, religious art, daily Christian living, etc.

2a) Episcopal Reception of these Expressions of Faith:
The bishops, immersed in the life of the Church, receive these faith expressions and assess their fidelity to the apostolic tradition.

4a) Reception of Doctrinal Formulations:
The Christian faithful engage this official teaching and, upon recognizing its fidelity to the lived faith of the Church, actively appropriate the new formulation. This, in turn, leads to new expressions of faith (1b).

3a) Official Formulation as Doctrine:
The bishops, if the need arises, give doctrinal form to the insights manifested in the faith expressions of the community.

The central distinction between this model and the juridical model is this: the juridical model sees the relationship between the bishops and the whole people of God moving in only one direction: from the bishops to the people. The *communio*-model offers instead a reciprocal give and take between the bishops and the community. The Church travels through history, expressing its faith in each new epoch in a kind of spiraling movement. Moreover, reception happens in two moments in this model. The first occurs as the bishops receive the faith of the people [from (1a) to (2a)], and the second occurs as the faithful receive the doctrinal formulations of the bishops [(3a) to (4a)].

In the first moment we begin not with laws and doctrines but with the lived experience and testimony of the Christian community (1a). This reflects the historical origins of church doctrine. The starting point was not doctrine but the testimony of the apostolic community of faith. Sacred texts, liturgical practices and the daily testimony of believers were the original depository of early Christian belief. Even later in the history of the Church we can recognize the way in which many church doctrines were first manifested in the lived faith of the people. For example, both Marian dogmas (the Immaculate Conception and the Bodily Assumption of Mary) emerged from the devotional life of the Church, in the prayer of the people, before they were formally proposed as doctrine. This model suggests that the process of doctrinal teaching actually begins with the magisterium *receiving* the lived faith of the people prior to its giving that faith any official formulation in law, ritual or doctrine.

What is often seen as a merely pragmatic process, namely, episcopal consultation, is in fact a vital exercise in ecclesial reception—the bishops "receive" the apostolic faith that emerges from the achieved consensus of the Church (*consensus fidelium*). The noted ecclesiologist and ecumenist, the late Jean-Marie Tillard, wrote that the bishop is "entrusted with the task of *watching over* the way the gift of God is *received* and passed on from one group to the other, one generation to the other."[6] Thus the bishop becomes the minister responsible for serving the "memory" of the Church.

This first moment of reception will lead to the second moment of reception [(3a) to (4a)] in which the formal teaching of the bishops is received and assimilated into the life of the Church. When the bishops deem it necessary, they give authoritative expression to the faith of the Church. Often the faith testimony of the Church was only implicit and undeveloped. Consequently, the bishops' formal teaching will be faithful to what is received while also adding to the faith of the Church in the process of formal expression. The authoritative teaching of the bishops is then received back by the churches. But the people's reception of episcopal teaching will be more than a passive act of obedience. In receiving that teaching and making it their own, the people will achieve new insight, new imaginative construals of their faith and will inevitably give that faith a new expression in their piety, art and in the concrete practice of Christian living.

This new reception of episcopal teaching will often occur in new cultural contexts, with new questions and expectations. The result of this new reception will be "a fresh remembrance," a "rediscovery" of neglected elements of the apostolic faith discovered from within new and unanticipated perspectives.[7] This is what gives this model its "spiraling" movement. For the reception of the episcopal teaching by the churches will, in turn, give rise to new expressions (1b) which may yield new official formulations [(2b–3b)] which in turn may or may not be received in the life of the Church (4b).

BECOMING A COMMUNITY OF DIALOGUE AND DISCERNMENT

The model of ecclesial reception offered above strives to honor two ecclesial realities: (1) the unique role of the bishops as those distinctly empowered within the Church to offer authoritative determinations of the apostolic faith, and (2) the role of the whole people of God who share in the process of hearing and giving expression to the Word of God as its subtle reverberations are discerned in the received tradition and the ongoing life of the Church.

This vision of the Church will not, as its critics might fear, undermine the legitimate authority of the pope and bishops. To the contrary, human experience tells us time and again that teachers who dare to listen and learn, always teach with greater authority. When the critics of Jesus asked by what authority he taught and ministered, the answer was clear. Jesus taught and acted as one consumed by the will of God. So too, popes and bishops rightly claim to teach with an authority that comes from the Spirit of God. But that Spirit speaks not through supernaturally infused knowledge, nor, ordinarily, through ecstatic vision. The Spirit of God must be heard in the testimony of the Scriptures and the living tradition of the Church manifested, in large part, in the testimony of the entire believing community.

The council, I believe, was haltingly nudging the Church beyond the rigid demarcation between a teaching church and a learning church, to a new vision of the Church as a community of dialogue and discernment. This is reflected in the following passage from *Gaudium et spes:*

. . . the church shows itself as a sign of that amity which renders possible sincere dialogue and strengthens it. Such a mission requires us first
of all to create in the church itself mutual esteem, reverence and har-
mony, and to acknowledge all legitimate diversity; in this way all who
constitute the one people of God will be able to engage in ever more
fruitful dialogue, whether they are pastors or other members of the
faithful. For the ties which unite the faithful together are stronger than
those which separate them: let there be unity in what is necessary, freedom in what is doubtful, and charity in everything (GS #92).

This passage offers a bracing image of the Church as a community
that dares the risk of charitable dialogue, not out of a rejection of legitimate authority but in order that legitimate authority might be more
fruitfully exercised within the Church. Pope Paul VI shared such a vision as well in his first encyclical, *Ecclesiam suam*. In that document,
authored while the council was still in progress, the pope made the
theme of dialogue the centerpiece of his reflection on the Church.

This vision of the Church as a community of dialogue will reject
the tendency to play the hierarchy off of the laity or to appeal to the
sense of the faithful as a mere counter-position to official church teaching. Those who embrace this vision of the Church will insist that the
"sense of the faithful" includes the whole faithful, cleric and lay. Consequently, they will reject any idea that the sense of the faithful represents some opposition party gathering in protest outside the walls of
church leadership. Rather, the sense of the faithful emerges with full
vitality when the whole Church dares to embrace that eschatological
modesty most becoming of a pilgrim Church, a Church that believes
that it abides in the truth but does not possess it in its entirety. This
pilgrim Church will be faithful to its truest identity when all the
baptized—pope, bishop and layperson—acknowledge the wisdom of
listening before speaking, of learning before teaching, of praying before pronouncing. In the humility of such a community, the Good
News of Jesus Christ will reverberate with an unimagined clarity and
power before a world hungry for a word of salvation.

DISPUTED QUESTIONS

1) Some church commentators have pointed out that the
spiritual sense of the faith given to each believer in baptism must
be cultivated within the life of the Church. One would assume,

they suggest, that Catholic Christians who have cultivated their spiritual instincts through the faithful practice of their Catholic faith will exercise a more developed insight than "lapsed" Catholics. Consequently, some have criticized appeals to polling data on the grounds that such polls seldom distinguish between active, practicing Catholics and inactive Catholics. Recourse to polls may be helpful but they are not sufficient for assessing the true sense of the faithful.

Other theologians respond that there are also dangers in offering a too strict definition of who constitutes "the faithful." In doing so one risks excluding the voices of persons who may be marginalized within the Church (the uneducated, persons of color, etc.) and/or find themselves, for various reasons, living in "ecclesial exile."

FOR FURTHER READING

Anglican-Roman Catholic Dialogue (ARCIC II), "The Gift of Authority," *Origins* 29 (May 27, 1999) 17–29.

Burkhard, John. "*Sensus Fidei*: Meaning, Role and Future of a Teaching of Vatican II." *Louvain Studies* 17 (1992) 18–34.

_____. "*Sensus Fidei:* Theological Reflection Since Vatican II." *Heythrop Journal* 34 (1993) 41–59, 137–59.

Congar, Yves. "Reception as an Ecclesiological Reality." In *Election and Consensus in the Church* {*Concilium* 77}. Giuseppe Alberigo and Anton Weiler, eds., 43–68. New York: Herder, 1972.

Espin, Orlando. *The Faith of the People: Theological Reflections on Popular Catholicism.* Maryknoll, N.Y.: Orbis, 1997.

Kilmartin, Edward. "Reception in History: An Ecclesiological Phenomenon and Its Significance." *Journal of Ecumenical Studies* 21 (1984) 34–54.

Metz, Johann Baptist and Edward Schillebeeckx, eds. *The Teaching Authority of the Believers* [*Concilium* #180] Edinburgh: T&T Clark, 1985.

Pottmeyer, Hermann J. "Reception and Submission." *The Jurist* 51 (1991) 269–92.

Rausch, Thomas. "Reception, Past and Present." *Theological Studies* 47 (1986) 497–508.

Rush, Ormond. *The Reception of Doctrine: An Appropriation of Hans Robert Jauss' Reception Aesthetics and Literary Hermeneutics.* Rome: Gregoriana, 1997.

_____. "*Sensus Fidei*: Faith 'Making Sense' of Revelation." *Theological Studies* 62 (June, 2001) 231–61.

EIGHT ===================================

IS THERE A PLACE FOR DISAGREEMENT IN THE CATHOLIC CHURCH?

The question that serves as the title of this chapter is one that has been addressed to me, in one form or another, on numerous occasions. It deserves a careful response. Some would read the question with a cynical eye, seeing it as reflective of the "cafeteria Catholicism" born out of an individualistic and consumerist culture. Others might note more hopefully that the question reflects a continued interest in preserving meaningful Catholic identity—no small thing in our world today.

If, as I have suggested earlier in the book, we respond to revelation first as an encounter with God, then the question of Catholic identity cannot be reduced to the question of allegiance to one or another of the Church's teachings. Catholic identity ought to be shaped by a willingness to be addressed by God in Christ by the power of the Spirit. That address comes in the form of authoritative church teaching to be sure. But identity as Catholic Christians who have been addressed by the God of Love ought also to be shaped by the narratives of the Christian faith: the biblical stories of those who first gave witness to the God of Love and the inspiring testimony of great saints who have not just taught but demonstrated with their lives what identifying oneself as a disciple of Christ might mean. Catholic identity ought to be shaped by the faithful celebration of the Eucharist that invites participants to enter into the paschal mystery of Christ and then sends them forth in mission. Catholic identity ought to be formed by regular engagement in the distinctive practices of the Church: fasting and feasting, almsgiving, visiting the sick, keeping the Sabbath, speaking out against

121

injustice. Only when we consider Catholic identity in these terms can we properly address the question of this chapter.

But address it we must, if only because our generation has seen an unprecedented expansion of the exercise of the Church's teaching office. No other generation in the history of the Church has been subject to the number of catechisms, directories, encyclicals, episcopal letters and curial instructions that we have seen in the last fifty years. "Church teaching" no longer means simply the creed; it has expanded to include questions on the morality of *in vitro* fertilization, the approved recipes for eucharistic bread and the morality of first use of nuclear weapons. Never before has Catholic Christianity exercised its teaching authority on such specific matters. Determining an adequate response to such an expansive exercise of church teaching authority has become necessary today more than ever before.

DISCERNING THE APPROPRIATE RESPONSE TO CHURCH TEACHING

In chapter seven we considered four basic gradations in the authority of church teaching. It follows that, if the centrality and authoritative status of church teaching differs, the response of believers to these various teachings will also differ.

The Appropriate Response to Church Dogma

Catholicism holds that dogmas are the most authoritative of church teachings for the simple reason that they mediate divine revelation, the substance of God's saving offer to humankind. Since dogmas mediate God's gift of self to humankind, the only appropriate response of a believer to dogma is what Vatican II called an "assent of faith." Faith is our most basic response to the revelation of God's love to us.

So how do we address the situation in which a Catholic Christian finds that they are unable to offer an assent of faith to a particular dogma? Roman Catholicism has traditionally held that, due to the central role that dogma plays in communicating God's saving Word, membership in the Church of Jesus Christ would be called into question by the obstinate and public denial of dogma. This kind of formal rejection is called *heresy*. However, formal heresy is, I believe, fairly rare. The actual stance of most Roman Catholics to at least some of the dogmatic teachings proposed by the Church falls somewhere between explicit affirmation and explicit rejection.

Most of the Church's central dogmatic teachings are found in the creeds or are embedded in the liturgical and sacramental life of the Church. Beyond these central teachings a student of the history of dogma might offer other dogmatic pronouncements defined by popes or councils to deal with important historical threats to the integrity of the Church's faith. At one point in history these dogmatic statements were vital to the Church's life, yet many have now faded from view, not because they are not true but rather because they are addressing questions that nobody is asking today.

Many Catholic Christians, secure in their fundamental profession of faith in Jesus Christ, will never find reason to consider many teachings that have dogmatic status. Questions regarding the existence of angels, the belief in Purgatory, the question of whether Christ has one or two wills—these matters will never trouble some believers. To say that they have given these teachings an explicit assent of faith would be misleading, as would the claim that they are denying them simply because their faith life has not demanded that they take up some of these specific teachings one way or another. In this situation, the stance of the believer can hardly be characterized as obstinate and public rejection.

It is still necessary to affirm that within the Roman Catholic tradition church dogma has a special claim on the faith of church members. Explicit rejection of a dogma of the Catholic Church would not necessarily place one outside the sphere of God's saving grace, but at some point such a denial might place one outside the Roman Catholic communion.

The Appropriate Response to Definitive Doctrine

The second category of church teaching that we have considered, definitive doctrine, includes teachings that do not themselves mediate divine revelation but are necessary to safeguard and expound revelation. Since definitive doctrine does not mediate divine revelation, there can be no question of a response of faith. Official church documents teach that the believer is bound to "firmly accept and hold as true" those teachings proposed as *definitive doctrines*. I find no evidence in tradition that the denial of definitive doctrine has ever been viewed as heresy in the modern sense of the word. Consequently, the rejection of a definitive doctrine would not seem to demand the same consequences as the denial of a dogma of the Church. Provided that one's rejection were well informed and in keeping with a firm desire to be united with the faith of the Church, the withholding of an internal assent from such a teaching, although potentially a serious error against the teaching of the Church, would not necessarily place one outside the Roman Catholic communion.

The Appropriate Response to Authoritative Doctrine

Many of the Church's teachings, particularly regarding the moral life, are examples of authoritative doctrine. Making sense of the appropriate response to such teaching is complicated by the fact that there is an implicit admission of the possibility of error, however remote. The response of believers to such teaching may have to take that possibility into account. According to Vatican II, Catholics are expected to give "a religious docility *(obsequium)* of the will and intellect" (LG #25) to the many teachings that fall in the third category of *authoritative doctrine*. The precise meaning of this phrase has been a matter of great debate. The key Latin word is *obsequium,* which is variously translated as "obedience," "submission," "docility," "due respect" or "assent." In truth, the Latin term can embrace all of these different senses.

Although there are sharp disagreements on this question, I would propose that the appropriate response to authoritative doctrine requires the believer to make a genuine effort to assimilate the given teaching into their personal religious convictions. In so doing, the believer is attempting to give an "internal assent" to the teaching. In the vast majority of cases, a believer will do so naturally and without any difficulty. Most Catholic Christians readily assent to the teachings of the Church, even where infallibility is not invoked. Often they do not go through any explicit process of analyzing the arguments underlying a particular teaching. They accept the teaching because they sense the intuitive "rightness" of the teaching or because they trust in the general authority of the Church's teaching office. Sometimes, however, this ready acceptance of authoritative doctrine does not happen. On occasion, a believer may face a particular teaching that, at least at first glance, seems problematic. Now what happens? In the language of Vatican II, what does "religious docility" demand in such a situation? I would propose three things.[1]

First, if I possess a religiously "docile" attitude to a problematic teaching I will be willing to engage in further study of the issue. Perhaps my questions are the consequence of poor or inadequate catechesis. Second, if the teaching in question regards matters of morality (e.g., cohabitation before marriage or recourse to artificial contraception), I ought to engage in an examination of conscience. This means asking myself some difficult questions regarding the nature of the difficulties I am having with a given teaching. Am I struggling with this teaching because I cannot discover in it the will of God, or is it because this teaching, if true, would demand some real conversion? Perhaps some basic aspect of my present lifestyle would have to change. Third, I must consider whether my difficulties lie not with a particular teaching but with the very idea of a church teaching office. To be a faithful Catholic is to accept the basic legitimacy of the Church's teaching office, even if one may have some objections about how that office is structured and exercised in practice.

This is a fairly demanding regimen, as it ought to be if I am to take issue with accepted church teaching. However, if I have had difficulties with a particular teaching and I have fulfilled these three steps and still cannot give an internal assent to that teaching I have done all the Church can ask of me and my inability to give an internal assent to this teaching does not in any way separate me from the Roman Catholic communion.

The Appropriate Response to Concrete Applications of Church Teaching, Prudential Admonitions and Church Discipline

Finally, the particular response that a believer owes to concrete applications of church teaching, prudential admonitions and church discipline could vary considerably. The American bishops recognized that, at the level of concrete applications of church teaching, it was possible for a Catholic to disagree with such applications in good conscience. Although the opinion of the bishops on such matters must be taken seriously, a Catholic does not have to agree, for example, with the bishops' specific policy proposals for improving the plight of the poor. The Catholic does have to accept the Church's teaching that every baptized Christian bears responsibility for the welfare of the poor.

Generally, we are called to accept the discipline of the Church as the "here and now" way in which the Church seeks to organize its concrete life. One can do so, moreover, even while questioning some of these disciplinary practices. To take an example from the civil order, I can think the speed limit for the streets in my neighborhood is too low but still obey the law. In the life of the Church, I can disagree with the laws of fasting and abstinence and still obey them.

There are times, however, when matters are not quite so simple. First, we can never follow a law when doing so would lead us to sin. Second, we must remember that church law does not exist for its own sake. Sometimes one is called to exercise the virtue of *epikeia*, that virtue which seeks what might be called "the spirit of the law." The practice of *epikeia* suggests that a law need not be obeyed if "its observance would be detrimental to the common good or the good of individuals."[2] It is worth remembering that church law exists to maintain church order, assist individual members in the call to holiness and further the mission of the Church. When the application of the law in a given instance does not demonstrably further these goals, it may yield to alternative actions that do further these goals.

To conclude this section, it may be helpful to line up the various responses demanded toward church teaching in the following chart:

LEVELS OF CHURCH TEACHING	RESPONSE OF THE BELIEVER
Dogma	**Assent of Faith** [The believer makes an act of faith, trusting that this teaching is revealed by God.]
Definitive Doctrine	**Firm Acceptance** [The believer "accepts and holds" these teachings to be true.]
Authoritative Doctrine	**"A Religious Docility of Will and Intellect"** [The believer strives to assimilate a teaching of the Church into their religious stance, while recognizing the remote possibility of church error.]
Provisional Applications of Church Doctrine, Church Discipline and Prudential Admonitions	**Conscientious Obedience** [The believer obeys (the spirit of) any church law or disciplinary action which does not lead to sin, even when questioning the ultimate value or wisdom of the law or action.]

Our faith in Jesus Christ is always greater than the sum total of the individual propositions and teachings to which we can give an assent. It is natural that our individual convictions will vary in the intensity of our commitment. We stake our life on the fundamentals of our faith, on our belief in God's saving love for us, a love which was incarnate in Jesus of Nazareth. At the same time, we acknowledge that as Christians we may be called upon—in humble reliance on the guidance of the Spirit—to stake out formal positions on the implications of the Gospel and the life of discipleship about which we cannot be absolutely certain. On the one hand, to remain silent might be an abdication of our responsibility to explore the specific demands of discipleship. On the other hand, to ignore the provisionality of some of these church positions, to act as if every formal teaching of the Church is equally central and lays the same claim on believers, is to be guilty of ecclesiastical hubris, a presumption to a kind of answer-book view of the Church's teaching office. This viewpoint is far removed from the approach of Vatican II which admitted that the Church did not have a ready answer to every question posed today (GS #33).

THE RESPONSIBILITIES OF THE PASTORAL MINISTER IN ASSISTING THOSE WHO STRUGGLE WITH CHURCH TEACHING

Pastoral ministers are often put in very difficult situations as they try to respond to individual Catholics who struggle with one or another of the Church's teachings. As *public* ministers, they are conscious of their responsibility to present faithfully the teaching of the Church. Their role is not identical with that of the professional theologian whose work is often more speculative and exploratory in its methodology and tentative in its conclusions. However, as *pastoral* ministers, they also wish to honor the real struggles of those to whom they minister. They know well that they are often ministering to adults with a deep and rich life of faith, many of whom are highly educated and accustomed to forming their own views—views which they expect to be taken seriously. In order to help pastoral ministers navigate this minefield successfully, I propose three basic responsibilities incumbent upon every pastoral minister in the presentation of church teaching.

The Responsibility to Present the Official Teaching
of the Church Comprehensively and Sympathetically

Every pastoral minister, ordained or lay, has the responsibility to present the official teaching of the Roman Catholic Church. This should be so obvious as to require no further comment. However, I am convinced that there is a great deal of misunderstanding regarding what this responsibility actually entails. No minister within the Church has the authority to offer an expurgated version of the Catholic faith. There is often the temptation to ignore those teachings of the Church that may present difficulties either for the minister or for those whom the minister is addressing. This temptation is understandable.

There are many faithful church ministers who are not equally comfortable with every teaching of the Church. In this situation, there is a tendency to avoid the topic altogether for fear of being in the position of (1) questioning church teaching in public, (2) defending church teaching without conviction, or (3) presenting church teaching in a superficial or haphazard fashion. For example, I once had a conversation with a priest ordained almost thirty years who said, with pride, that he had never publicly addressed the issue of artificial contraception in his priestly ministry. It was obvious from his comments that he had serious difficulties with the Church's position on this question. He is certainly not alone. However, is there not a latent paternalism here which assumes that the minister knows better than the one being ministered to which official positions of the Church are correct and which are not? The minister must remember that not everyone will share his/her personal difficulties, and that everyone has a right to a clear, comprehensive and sympathetic presentation of church teaching. For any minister to edit the Church's teaching because of personal difficulties is to let their own judgment replace that of those they are teaching.

Besides this latent paternalism, there are other factors that contribute to a selective presentation of the Catholic faith. One factor is the poor theological formation of church ministers, including many clergy. Too often a minister will struggle with an official teaching of the Church because of inadequate theological formation. Teachings on Mary, eschatology, original sin, eucharistic real presence, sexual morality etc. are often ignored because the minister finds popular/traditional treatments of the subject less than persuasive. Proper theological formation and ongoing education for ministry is absolutely essential. The minister must be able to present adequately the teaching of the Church in language and concepts intelligible to the modern Catholic.

The responsibility to present the teaching of the Church *comprehensively* risks being misunderstood if it is conceived as simply going through a checklist of doctrinal propositions. Rote memorization and repetition of formal doctrinal propositions is not catechesis. Formal dogmas and doctrines are summary statements, "bottom line" summations of a rich theological tradition. The Church's ministers require formal theological training precisely so that they can go beyond the mere repetition of doctrinal propositions. For example, contemporary models of catechesis in the catechumenate rightly begin, not with doctrinal propositions, but with the liturgy, liturgical calendar, creeds and lectionary. This leads us to the second responsibility of the public minister.

The Responsibility to Make Explicit, When Appropriate, the Binding Character of a Particular Teaching

In chapter 6 and again in this chapter we have stressed the importance of recognizing that there is a gradation in the authority of church teaching. Unfortunately, these distinctions were often considered of mere academic value. Many insisted (and many still do today) that the faithful need not be informed of the authoritative status of a teaching for fear of encouraging a "cafeteria Catholicism" where Catholics feel free to reject any doctrine that has not been proposed infallibly. Too often in contemporary preaching and catechesis there is scant consideration of the important gradations of authoritative church teaching. This attitude suggests yet another form of ecclesiastical paternalism. These distinctions have developed within the Catholic tradition for a reason: not everything the Church teaches is divinely revealed. Consequently, with regard to the Church's authoritative but non-defined teaching, there is at least a remote possibility of error. One can imagine pastoral situations in which it would be appropriate to inform an individual struggling with a given teaching of the relatively binding status of the teaching at issue.

How does the minister determine the authoritative status of a church teaching? This responsibility has traditionally been given to the community of theologians. Obviously, this meant theologians who were "in good standing" in the Church. In earlier times theologians would assess the form in which a teaching had been proposed (for example, solemn definitions might introduce a dogmatic statement with "I/we solemnly define and declare. . . ."), the authoritative status of the document within which a teaching was proposed (e.g., a constitution, encyclical, apostolic letter), the historical context out of which the teaching emerged, and the frequency with which it had been taught. The theologians would then offer their judgment regarding the authoritative status of that teaching, and that judgment would be included in theological manuals and catechisms. This tradition of assigning a particular "note" to a teaching has fallen into disuse. The lack of any alternative system creates special difficulties for the public minister. One can only hope that in the future, official catechetical materials will draw on the careful study of theologians and do a better job of explicitly stating the authoritative status of a given teaching.

The Responsibility to Offer Pastoral Guidance to Those Who Struggle with Church Teaching

What are the obligations of a minister when meeting with someone who seeks advice in confronting a difficult teaching? In these instances the task of pastoral ministers is not unlike that of the spiritual director. The task of the good spiritual director is to help the directee recognize the signposts on their particular journey of faith: it is not to chart their spiritual path for them. Where individuals come to a public minister of the Church with questions or difficulties regarding a church teaching, it is the task of the minister to guide them in the process of arriving at internal assent. This guidance would certainly include a fair presentation of the official teaching of the Church, including the theological arguments that have been proposed in support of this teaching. It may also be helpful to acknowledge opposing arguments while stressing that these arguments do not possess the same official or authoritative character.

Second, the minister must clarify the authoritative status of the particular teaching. Are we dealing with a central dogma of the faith (e.g., the bodily resurrection of Jesus) or with a particular teaching of the Church that, while authoritative, would have a significantly different status (e.g., the Church's position on tubal ligation when a woman is medically unable to bring a pregnancy to term)? Obviously, difficulties regarding the first example would be much more significant than those related to the second.

Third, the minister can invite the individual to an examination of conscience in order to ascertain whether the difficulties lie in a fear of the conversion that assent to a particular teaching (particularly in the area of morality) might demand. Finally, the minister can ask the individual to assess their attitude toward the authority of the ecclesiastical magisterium. In our society, particularly in this country, it is easy to fall prey to an attitude which sees any exercise of church authority as archaic or out of step with the times.

Having completed this process, the minister has fulfilled his or her responsibility to assist the individual in the proper formation and examination of conscience. The decision to give or withhold assent is placed where it rightly belongs, with the person who has the difficulties with the given teaching. In daily Christian living each believer must engage their conscience in concrete decisions for which they alone will be responsible before God. They must also take responsibility to see that their consciences are properly formed. In the Declaration on Religious Liberty, #14, Vatican II taught that, in the formation of conscience, the Christian faithful "*must pay careful attention* to the holy and certain teaching of the church." A number of bishops proposed an amendment in which the phrase ". . . must pay careful attention to. . . ." would be replaced by the passage ". . . ought to form their consciences according to. . . ." The theological commission responded that "the proposed formula seems excessively restrictive. The obligation binding upon the faithful is sufficiently expressed in the text as it stands."[3] The public minister must be mindful of the fact that he or she is presenting the teaching of the Church to responsible moral agents who alone will have to give or not give an assent to a particular teaching and engage their consciences on that basis.

It is possible that those with whom the minister is dealing will not want to assume their proper responsibility. They may want the minister to "give them permission" to reject a certain teaching. However, I do not believe this "permission" is the minister's to give. On the other hand, neither is it the place of the minister to pronounce judgment on the ultimate spiritual consequences of a failure to arrive at internal assent (e.g., "if you do not agree with the Church on this matter, you stand in peril of your salvation"). No minister of the Church, from the pope to the parish catechist, is empowered either *to command* assent to church teaching or *to dispense* from that assent, and no minister is empowered to pass formal judgment on the ultimate spiritual consequences of a particular stance toward church teaching.

Finally, the permissibility of withholding assent as a matter of conscience, in these carefully defined circumstances, must not be viewed by the minister as a mere act of condescension to human weakness and error. Because the magisterium itself grants the possibility of error in the proclamation of authoritative doctrine, the difficulties raised by believers may positively assist the Church in recognizing its error and moving forward in pursuit of the "plenitude of truth."

In the end, the ultimate responsibility of the public minister within the Catholic Church is to proclaim the Gospel of Jesus Christ as it finds expression in the Roman Catholic tradition. The minister proclaims church teaching comprehensively, sympathetically, and in a pastorally sensitive manner. At the same time the minister must always remember that responsibility for responding to that teaching lies with another. Every minister prays that they might be an instrument of the Holy Spirit. But that same Spirit works through those who seek to make the teaching of the Church their own, and *their* struggles, their often courageous attempts to grapple with the demands of church teaching, also constitute a valuable contribution to the life of the Church.

DISPUTED QUESTIONS

1) The category of definitive doctrine is a new one in the current taxonomy of church teaching. Many questions remain, not only regarding the scope of this category of church teaching but also regarding the consequences for not giving such teachings an internal assent. This remains an open question. In a commentary on the Profession of Faith, Cardinal Ratzinger and Archbishop Bertone claimed that those who fail to give an internal assent to a definitive doctrine are not "in full communion." The language employed is ambiguous at best. For example, it is not clear whether those who do not give an internal assent to these teachings would be excluded from the sacraments.

2) In this chapter we have generally discussed the situation in which a believer cannot give an "internal assent" to a particular teaching. One sometimes comes across the language of

"dissent" to describe this situation. I generally prefer to reserve the term dissent for public statements of disagreement with church teaching. The status of one's internal assent is a matter of individual conscience. When one "dissents" from a teaching, one is making one's disagreement public. Current ecclesiastical documents tend to give more leeway to the possibility of privately withholding assent than they do to the legitimacy of public dissent.

Many church officials believe that public dissent is always inappropriate. Others contend that the legitimacy of public dissent depends in large part on underlying motive. If the dissent is motivated by a desire to discredit the teaching office of the Church, then such actions would not be in keeping with authentic church membership. If, however, such public dissent is engaged in with proper respect for church tradition and the Church's teaching office, it is conceivable that such public action might become an instrument of the Spirit in effecting necessary reform and renewal in the Church. The question of dissent among theologians will be handled in the next chapter.

FOR FURTHER READING

Congregation for the Doctrine of the Faith. "Profession of Faith and Oath of Fidelity." *Origins* 18 (March 16, 1989) 661, 663.

Curran, Charles E. and Richard A. McCormick, eds. *Readings in Moral Theology No. 6: Dissent in the Church.* New York: Paulist, 1988.

Gaillardetz, Richard R. Chapter 5 in *Teaching with Authority: A Theology of the Magisterium in the Church,* 255–73. Collegeville: The Liturgical Press, 1997.

Ratzinger, Cardinal Joseph, and Archbishop Tarcisio Bertone. "Commentary on Profession of Faith's Concluding Paragraphs." *Origins* 28 (July 16, 1998) 116–19.

Sullivan, Francis A. *Magisterium: Teaching Office in the Catholic Church.* New York: Paulist, 1983.

NINE

WHAT IS THE PROPER
RELATIONSHIP BETWEEN
THE MAGISTERIUM
AND THEOLOGIANS?

The popular view of the relationship between the magisterium and theologians in the North American church is not positive. One reads in the newspaper of "dissenting" theologians and doctrinal "witch hunts" conducted by church officials. The overall sense communicated to the public is of a relationship characterized by suspicion and animosity. Certainly there are some tensions, but I think the public perception is somewhat distorted. It does not take into account the many bishops who hold theologians in high esteem and consult them regularly. It does not consider the theologians who assist the various committees and sub-committees of the bishops' conference or serve as delegates on the many formal ecumenical dialogues sponsored by the bishops' conference or even the Vatican. The public is generally not aware of the serious attempts of the various professional societies in theology, canon law and biblical studies to work collaboratively with the bishops on projects of mutual concern. These things do not find their way into newspapers because they are not provocative.

I am not suggesting that the relationship between the magisterium and theologians is without problems. I do believe that at least some of these problems are the consequence of the contemporary Church's failure to consider the full ramifications of Vatican II's teaching. That teaching, as with so many areas of church life, challenged the view of the magisterium—theologian relationship dominant on the eve of the council.

THE PRE-CONCILIAR VIEW OF THE
MAGISTERIUM—THEOLOGIAN RELATIONSHIP

The decades since the close of the council have seen a shift in our understanding of the relationship between bishops and theologians. Before the Second Vatican Council many ecclesiastical documents viewed theology as an auxiliary service to the ecclesiastical magisterium. In this view Peter and the apostles were sent forth by Christ with a unique teaching mission and were promised the assistance of the Holy Spirit. The pope and bishops were the successors to this teaching mission and also shared in the assistance of the Holy Spirit such that they, and they alone, were the authoritative teachers of the Church. The pope and bishops belonged to the "teaching church," and everyone else, including theologians, belonged to the "learning church." This view of teaching authority fit well with the more propositional view of revelation that was dominant in the decades prior to the council. Divine revelation was construed as a set of fixed propositional truths that quantitatively comprised the deposit of faith. The pope and bishops were the sole custodians and authoritative transmitters of that deposit.

Within this framework the role of theologians was reduced to explicating the meaning of these propositional truths. The teaching ministry of theologians, such as it was, was totally dependent on the authority of the pope and bishops. Theologians could be seen as teachers of the faith only by virtue of a delegation of authority from the bishops. They were expected to submit their work to the authoritative scrutiny and potential censorship of the magisterium. "Dissent," understood as the rejection or even questioning of any authoritative teaching of the magisterium, was viewed with suspicion as a negative attack on the authority of the magisterium itself. Of course, this was not absolute. The dogmatic manuals acknowledged the legitimacy of limited speculative discussion that was critical of certain doctrinal formulations. However, the assumption was that if theologians discovered a significant difficulty with a doctrinal formulation that had not been proposed infallibly, they were to bring the difficulty to the attention of the hierarchy in private, and to refrain from any public speech or writing that was contrary to received church teaching.

In sum, the basic dynamic of the magisterium-theologian relationship moved uni-directionally from the pope and bishops to the theologians (see figure below).

Pre-Conciliar View of the Magisterium-Theologian Relationship

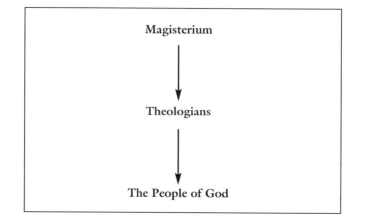

Even prior to the opening of Vatican II, important elements of this conception of the magisterium-theologian relationship were beginning to be questioned. New developments in the theology of revelation challenged the somewhat simplistic conception of the transmission of church teaching as the handing on of a collection of individual truths. Moreover, there did not seem to be a sufficient acknowledgement of the role of the Holy Spirit in the life of the whole Church. The dominant conception of the Church itself was excessively pyramidal and consequently saw revelation as "trickling down" from the hierarchy, through the theologians to the laity.

VATICAN II'S NEW FRAMEWORK FOR CONSIDERING THE MAGISTERIUM— THEOLOGIAN RELATIONSHIP

The inadequacies of this understanding of the magisterium-theologian relationship were brought to light in the teaching of Vatican II. The council presented divine revelation as the living Word of God communicated in its fullness by the power of the Holy Spirit in the person of Jesus Christ. This Word was addressed not exclusively to Peter and the apostles or the pope and bishops but to the whole Church and, indeed, to all humankind. The magisterium was to be a servant to this Word as its authoritative interpreter. In this regard, the vocation of bishops and theologians shared a common foundation, service to the Word of God.

Unlike the pre-conciliar view, the council did not limit the work of the Spirit to ensuring the efficacy of the sacraments and empowering church office. The bishops envisioned a Church wholly animated by the Spirit, a recipient of both "hierarchic and charismatic" gifts. The introduction of the biblical concept of "charism" opened up the possibility that theologians might exercise their work, not by way of delegation, but by the exercise of a charism vital to the building up of the Church in faith. Finally, the council's teaching that the Church did not have all truth as its possession but rather moved toward the "fullness of truth" (DV #8) suggested a prominent role for theologians in the ecclesial work of reflection and discovery as the Church journeyed toward the fullness of truth.

The council did not reflect explicitly on the role of the theologian in any depth. However, several passages are worth considering. The bishops insisted that the work of biblical exegesis and theology must be done under the guidance of the magisterium:

> Catholic exegetes . . . and other students of sacred theology, working diligently together and using appropriate means, should devote their energies, under the watchful care of the sacred teaching office of the Church, to an exploration and exposition of the divine writings (DV #23).

They reiterated that it was the responsibility of theologians to interpret and explicate church teaching faithfully. However these tasks did not exhaust the work of theologians. Theologians must also consider new questions:

> . . . recent research and discoveries in the sciences, in history and philosophy bring up new problems which have an important bearing on life itself and demand new scrutiny by theologians. Furthermore, theologians are now being asked, within the methods and limits of theological science, to develop more efficient ways of communicating doctrine to the people of today. . . . (GS #64).

Though the council texts did not develop this, the work of the theologian is presented as a mediation between insights gained from a study of the contemporary situation and the probing interpretation of the received church tradition. In several other texts the bishops encouraged theologians to explore unresolved doctrinal questions (LG #54, and the *Nota praevia explicativa* #4). Finally, the council reminded theologians of the importance of keeping in mind the ecumenical dimensions of their work (UR #10).

POST-CONCILIAR REFLECTION

In the years after the close of Vatican II, the International Theological Commission (ITC), newly created by Pope Paul VI, explored in a much more systematic manner many of the themes tentatively touched upon in the council. In 1975 they issued a document entitled *Theses on the Relationship between the Ecclesiastical Magisterium and Theology*,[1] which sought to apply the teachings of the council specifically to the question of the proper relationship between the magisterium and theologians. The ITC presented the work of theologians as a two-way mediation between the magisterium and the people of God.[2] With reference to the magisterium, the theological community tries to ensure that the authentic teaching of the Church is communicated as clearly and effectively as possible. With respect to the people of God, the theological community discerns the unique insights of all the baptized and gives these systematic expression. What was most striking about this document was the way the commission further developed the council's tentative shift from the descending, pre-conciliar model of the magisterium-theologian relationship. The document offered in its place a much more cooperative and dialogical view of the relationship between the theologians and the bishops.

Since the publication of the ITC document, two other documents have appeared that address the relationship between the theological community and the magisterium. In 1989 the American bishops, in collaboration with the Catholic Theological Society of America and the Canon Law Society of America, promulgated the document *Doctrinal Responsibilities: Approaches to Promoting Cooperation and Resolving Misunderstandings between Bishops and Theologians*.[3] This document drew heavily on the earlier ITC document as it sought to provide guidelines for resolving disputes between the bishops and theologians. In 1990, the CDF issued its own document, "Instruction on the Ecclesial Vocation of the Theologian."[4] Though they are not equally successful in this regard, all three documents share the new ecclesiological foundation established by Vatican II; all three documents situate the ministries of both the magisterium and the theological community within the larger context of the people of God.[5] Drawing on an ecclesiology of communion, these documents all reflect the conviction that the Word of God is the private possession of neither the magisterium nor the theologians but resides in the whole Church. Cardinal Ratzinger, in his commentary on the CDF instruction, drew attention to this fact:

> Looking at the articulation of the document, one is almost struck by the fact that we have not introduced it by speaking first about the magisterium, but rather about the topic of truth as a gift from God to his people. The truth of faith is not given to isolated individuals; rather through it God wanted to give life to a history and to a people. The truth is located in the communitarian subject of the People of God.[6]

Ratzinger sees in the CDF document a shift from a "'magisterium-theology' dualism" to a "triangular relationship: the People of God, as the bearer of the sense of faith and as the place common to all in the ensemble of faith, Magisterium and theology."[7] This triangular relationship (see figure below), I believe, better reflects the proper role of the community of theologians in the process of ecclesial reception.

DIALOGICAL MODEL OF MAGISTERIUM— THEOLOGIAN RELATIONSHIP

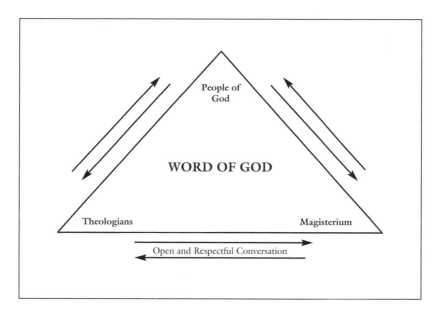

The CDF describes the role of the theologian in this way:

> His role is to pursue in a particular way an ever deeper understanding of
> the word of God found in the inspired Scriptures and handed on by the
> living tradition of the church. He does this in communion with the
> magisterium, which has been charged with the responsibility of pre-
> serving the deposit of faith.[8]

The theological community seeks this "deeper understanding" of God's
Word by employing the appropriate scholarly tools along two axes.
The first axis is historical and entails reflection on what David Tracy
calls the great "classics" of the tradition (e.g., the Scriptures, doctrinal
statements, theological treatises, ritual actions and symbols). The proper
application of the scientific tools for historical study will be critical to
the successful retrieval of the apostolic faith as it is encountered in its
many and diverse historical expressions. At this point specialists in biblical and historical studies will have a particularly significant contribution to make.

The second axis considers the diverse testimony of communities of
faith at the present moment, each striving to address the pressing concerns and insights of their particular communities. Theologians must
be in critical conversation with these communities, assisting them in
interpreting "the signs of the times," and helping to discover the unique
insights that these communities offer regarding the Christian faith in
the present moment. Among its many tasks and responsibilities, theology must help facilitate a conversation between the historical expressions of the Christian faith and the new insights and questions of the
people of God today.

Finally, I should note that all three post-conciliar documents affirmed, again in differing degrees, the critical dimension of the theological enterprise. The International Theological Commission wrote:

> [T]he theologian's task of interpreting the statements of the past and
> present magisterium, of putting them into the context of the whole of
> revealed truth, and of seeking a better understanding of them with the
> aid of the science of hermeneutics, brings with it a function that is in
> some sense critical. This criticism, of course, must be of the positive,
> not the destructive kind.[9]

It is the recognition of this critical task, more than anything else, that
differentiates this view of the theological vocation from that dominant

immediately before Vatican II. There is an acknowledgment here, however tentative, that constructive theological criticism need not be a sign of disloyalty but a genuine service to the Church.[10]

DEALING WITH CONFLICTS

The ministry of theologians shares with the ministry of the bishops a common commitment to the Word of God, but the principal responsibility of the bishops is to safeguard the integrity of the apostolic faith. This means that the magisterium is, by definition, conservative. I do not use the word "conservative" here in its ideological sense (conservative as opposed to liberal) but in its most fundamental meaning. As Francis Sullivan has observed

> its [the magisterium] primary function is not to penetrate into the depths of the mysteries of faith (the task of theology) but rather to safeguard the priceless treasure of the word of God and to defend the purity of the faith of the Christian community.[11]

The work of the theological community is, by its nature, more tentative and experimental than that of the bishops. It is oriented toward deepening the Church's apprehension and assimilation of that faith. Frequently, when a theologian publishes a work, the assumption is not that she is offering the final word on a topic but that she is offering an approach or insight to the theological community for its assessment. Anyone who has attended a serious theological conference knows that the community of theologians takes this responsibility very seriously. Major theological contributions are invariably subject to intense academic scrutiny. The best theologians welcome the critical conversation that ensues upon the publication of their views for they view each publication, not as a definitive pronouncement, but as the contribution toward a larger work in progress. Those who argue that the magisterium has an obligation to take an aggressive, interventionist stance in policing the work of theologians overlook the effective way in which the theological community assesses its own productions. Recently, at an annual theological convention, I attended a session in which a noted and somewhat controversial theologian gave a lively response to over thirty critical reviews of his new book!

Frequently, when a theologian makes a new contribution to his field, the critical give and take among his fellow scholars revolves around the fruitfulness of the particular line of inquiry taken in the work. Scholars might criticize the interpretation of historical data or the methodology employed. Occasionally theologians will find it necessary to make their own judgments regarding the congruence of a particular theological work with the official teaching of the Church. They do so with the humble recognition that all theological reflection falls short in some decisive way in the face of the incomprehensible mystery of God.

Even granting the work that theologians do to assess their colleagues' writings, Catholic teaching holds that the pope and bishops bear ultimate responsibility for determining whether a theological work is congruent with the received teaching of the Church. But how ought that judgment to be exercised?

History suggests that the most effective exercise of doctrinal judgment must be undertaken judiciously and with great prudence. Some of the saddest episodes in the history of the Church have occurred when overzealous holders of church office entered into premature and/or ill-informed judgment of a theologian's work. Consequently, one of the most significant exercises of doctrinal judgment by the Church's teaching office may be the *refusal* to offer a doctrinal judgment at all! In the sixteenth and seventeenth centuries there was a notorious dispute between the Jesuits and the Dominicans regarding the relationship between divine initiative and human freedom. After considerable theological debate and a series of ecclesiastical investigations, Pope Paul V's exercise of doctrinal judgment consisted in prohibiting either side from condemning the views of the other. This papal act implicitly acknowledged the difficult and speculative theological issues being considered and the need for theologians to have some freedom in probing the mysterious interplay of divine initiative and human freedom. Of course, formal condemnations are occasionally necessary, but they ought to be the instrument of last resort in the fulfillment of the magisterium's unique responsibility for safeguarding the faith.

One sometimes hears the complaint that Catholic theologians today present themselves as a "competing magisterium" to that of the college of bishops. It is a caricature that gains credence more by its widespread repetition than by any objective analysis of the situation in the Church today. I personally know of no serious Catholic theologian who holds that they possess the same authority as that of the college of bishops. Indeed, in my experience the vast majority of

Catholic theologians recognize the unique role that the bishops play in the life of the Church. They acknowledge a legitimate accountability to the ecclesiastical magisterium even as they may disagree with the concrete manner in which ecclesiastical oversight, in particular instances, is exercised.

I suspect that the dangers posed by "dissenting" theologians have been a little exaggerated. Credentialed Catholic theologians are readily identified, and to the extent that they speak in public or publish their views, are easily held accountable for their fidelity to the great tradition of the Church. If a particular theologian proposes a position clearly at variance with church teaching, the Church's teaching office should make a straightforward statement to the effect that position x proposed by theologian y does not, at present, represent the accepted teaching of the Church. This it does in order to assist those who, lacking scholarly expertise, might be misled regarding the status of a given theological perspective. However, it is quite another thing to brand a scholar indiscriminately as a "dissenting theologian." A theologian might, in the course of her work, offer a view point that in the judgment of the magisterium is not in accord with church teaching. That hardly means that everything that theologian writes or says must be held suspect. It goes without saying that in a Christian community committed to the principles of justice and charity, rigorous standards of due process and the determination to read a theologian's work in the best possible light will govern any necessary doctrinal investigation.

In this volume the question of authority has been consistently situated within a theological vision of the Church as a spiritual communion of persons bound together by a common faith and a common love of God. A Church that dares to call itself a community of disciples of Jesus of Nazareth must make charitable and respectful dialogue, and a willingness to both give and receive fraternal correction, the hallmarks of its communal existence.

DISPUTED QUESTIONS

1) Important questions are being raised in the Church today regarding the role of dissent in the work of the theologian. The CDF document "Instruction on the Ecclesial Vocation of the Theologian" allowed for the possibility that a theologian might

not be able to give an internal assent to an authoritative teaching of the magisterium. It assumed however, that in such cases, the theologian must communicate their concerns to the appropriate church authorities and then, if necessary, "suffer in silence." The CDF condemned the practice of "public dissent." If theologians were allowed to dissent publicly from church teaching, they would undermine the authority of the Church's teaching office and cause confusion among the faithful regarding the reliability of church teaching.

This rejection of public dissent has been widely criticized. First, there is the question of what constitutes public dissent. Is the publication of a scholarly article critical of an authoritative teaching of the Church "public dissent" or does "public dissent" mean organized and antagonistic resistance to the Church's teaching office? The CDF appears to have had in mind the latter more than the former but it was not as clear on this question as one would like. More importantly, if one recognizes that there is a possibility of error, however remote, in the exercise of the ordinary magisterium, then might not the respectful "public dissent" of theologians be an instrument of the Spirit for necessary change?

2) At the urging of the Vatican, in 2001 the American bishops passed juridical norms for the implementation of Pope John Paul II's *Ex corde ecclesiae*, an apostolic constitution on Catholic higher education. Those norms required that Catholic theologians teaching the "sacred sciences" at a Catholic institution must request a *mandatum* from their local bishop declaring that they teach Catholic doctrine as the authoritative position of the Church. This requirement has been a matter of no small controversy and as this book goes to press, it is still too early to know how this policy will be implemented. Defenders of this policy see it as nothing more than "truth in advertising." Students and parents of students have a right to know whether faculty members at a Catholic institution are teaching the official doctrine of the Catholic Church. The *mandatum* does not impinge upon academic freedom. It merely ensures that Catholic theologians will not teach speculative opinions as the official teaching of the Church.

Critics of this policy see it as a return to the kind of "ecclesiastical McCarthyism" that followed the condemnations of modernism at the beginning of the twentieth century. They fear that the procedures for granting or withholding the *mandatum* will not be conducted uniformly and that what constitutes "full communion" with the Church will be interpreted quite differently from bishop to bishop. Many fear that the decision not to seek a *mandatum* may unfairly brand some theologians as heterodox.

FOR FURTHER READING

Boyle, John P. *Church Teaching Authority: Historical and Theological Studies,* 142–60, 171–75. Notre Dame, Ind.: University of Notre Dame Press, 1995.

Congregation for the Doctrine of the Faith. "Instruction on the Ecclesial Vocation of the Theologian," *Origins* 20 (July 5, 1990) 117–26.

Dulles, Avery. "Criteria of Catholic Theology." *Communio* 22 (1995) 303–15.

_____. "The Two Magisteria: An Interim Reflection." *Catholic Theological Society of America Proceedings* 34 (1980) 155–69.

Figueiredo, Anthony J. *The Magisterium—Theology Relationship: Contemporary Theological Conceptions in the Light of Universal Church Teaching Since 1835 and the Pronouncements of the Bishops of the United States.* Rome: Gregorian, 2001.

International Theological Commission. *Theses on the Relationship between the Ecclesiastical Magisterium and Theology.* In *Readings in Moral Theology No. 3.* Charles E. Curran and Richard A. McCormick, eds., 151–70. New York: Paulist, 1982.

Komonchak, Joseph. "The Magisterium and Theologians." *Chicago Studies* 29 (November, 1990) 307–29.

National Conference of Catholic Bishops. *Doctrinal Responsibilities: Approaches to Promoting Cooperation and Resolving Misunderstandings between Bishops and Theologians.* Washington, D.C.: U.S.C.C., 1989.

Sullivan, Francis A. "The Theologian's Ecclesial Vocation and the 1990 CDF Instruction." *Theological Studies* 52 (1991) 51–68.

EPILOGUE

Several themes have run throughout this volume. I have consistently drawn on a theology of revelation that is trinitarian and sees the whole Church as the recipient of God's revelatory self gift in Jesus Christ by the power of the Holy Spirit. I have tried to maintain the delicate balance involved in affirming that the whole Church is both the recipient of this gift of revelation and the instrument through which the divine self-gift can continue to be made known to humankind. The second theme, perhaps less obvious, was that church authority is only intelligible within a community that holds to the belief that ultimate authority lies in God alone. The authentic exercise of authority within the community of faith depends on this vital conviction that God is the only ultimate spiritual authority in our lives and that all other "church authorities" are but limited mediations of divine authority. Words like "inerrancy" and "infallibility," while having a proper meaning and place in the Catholic Christian community, can mislead when they are used to absolutize some created authority, whether it is the Bible or the pope.

As Catholic Christians we "grant" authority to the Bible or the pope, fully aware that they share in a limited and imperfect though altogether necessary way in the authority of God. We hope for eternal communion with God but know that to live in history is to live in an often ambiguous world in which the "Author" of our lives is encountered in fits and snatches, through creation, the face of the stranger, and the mediations of sacred texts and offices. We might wish that it were otherwise. We might long to get divine truth "straight from the horse's mouth," as it were. We might wistfully imagine a Bible where the fingerprints of flawed human authors were not so apparent. We might pine for church leaders who were always wise, prophetic and comforting, all at the same time. We might expect that baptized followers of Christ would imitate him a bit more closely. For that matter, we might wish that salvation had come in some other way than through an unlettered craftsman who never traveled more than a hundred miles from his obscure hometown and ended his grand movement executed on a cross. We might wish for these things. But we will cling to these modest, human instruments of divine authority nevertheless, because, though flawed, we recognize in them a precious and necessary connection to the one true "Author" of our lives.

NOTES

PREFACE

[1] M. D. Chenu, *Toward Understanding Saint Thomas* (Chicago: Henry Regency, 1964) 48.

INTRODUCTION

[1] For a fuller development of this understanding of revelation see, Avery Dulles, *Models of Revelation* (Garden City: Doubleday, 1983) 131–54.

[2] What follows is indebted to the lucid and concise treatment of human experience in Dermot Lane's *The Experience of God: An Invitation to Do Theology* (New York: Paulist, 1981) 4–9.

CHAPTER ONE

[1] Robert Gnuse, *The Authority of the Bible: Theories of Inspiration, Revelation and the Canon of Scripture* (New York: Paulist, 1985) 22–65.

CHAPTER TWO

[1] This brief summary of the history of the Bible is drawn from Christopher De Hamel, *The Book. A History of the Bible* (London: Phaidon Press, 2001).

[2] Ibid., 216.

[3] Michael Prokurat, "Orthodox Interpretation of Scripture," in *The Bible in the Churches,* edited by Kenneth Hagan, 3rd ed. (Milwaukee: Marquette University Press, 1998) 62.

[4] Ibid.

⁵ Robert Gnuse, *The Authority of the Bible: Theories of Inspiration, Revelation and the Canon of Scripture* (New York: Paulist, 1985) 110.

⁶ Albert Sundberg, "The Bible Canon and the Christian Doctrine of Inspiration," *Interpretation* (1974) 371.

⁷ Gnuse, 116–7.

⁸ James Barr, *The Scope and Authority of the Bible* (Philadelphia: Westminster Press, 1980) 60–61.

CHAPTER THREE

¹ I summarize Thiel's treatment in the following section, while adapting and simplifying some of his terminology. John Thiel, *Senses of Tradition: Continuity and Development in Catholic Faith* (New York: Oxford University Press, 2000) 31–160.

² *Discorsi Messagio Colloqui del S. Padre Giovanni XXIII*, vol. 2 (Città Vaticano, 1960–1967) 652, as quoted in Giuseppe Alberigo, "The Announcement of the Council," in *History of Vatican II*, vol. I, Giuseppe Alberigo and Joseph A. Komonchak, eds. (Maryknoll, N.Y.: Orbis, 1995) 53.

CHAPTER FOUR

¹ The classic essays on this topic are both by Yves Congar, "A Semantic History of the Term 'Magisterium'" and "A Brief History of the Forms of the Magisterium and its Relations with Scholars," in *Readings in Moral Theology No. 3: The Magisterium and Morality*, Charles E. Curran and Richard A. McCormick, eds. (New York: Paulist, 1982) 297–313 and 314–31.

² St. Cyprian of Carthage, *Epistle*, 14, 4.

³ St. Augustine, *Sermon*, 340.

⁴ St. Cyprian of Carthage, *Epistle*, 67, 4.

⁵ Richard A. McCormick, *Notes on Moral Theology: 1965 through 1980* (Lanham, Md.: University Press of America, 1981) 261ff.

⁶ Karl Rahner, "The Teaching Office of the Church in the Present-Day Crisis of Authority," in *Theological Investigations*, vol. 12 (New York: Seabury, 1974) 12.

⁷ Jerome Murphy-O'Connor, "Eucharist and Community in I Corinthians," in *Living Bread, Saving Cup*, Kevin Seasoltz, ed. (Collegeville: The Liturgical Press, 1982) 4.

⁸ Jean Jacques von Allmen, "L'Église locale parmi les autres églises locales," *Irénikon* 43 (1970) 512.

⁹ Margaret O'Gara has used the image of the "gift exchange" to describe ecumenical relations between different Christian communions. See Margaret O'Gara, *The Ecumenical Gift Exchange* (Collegeville: The Liturgical Press, 1998).

¹⁰ St. Ignatius of Antioch, *Epistle to the Romans*, 4.

¹¹ St. Irenaeus of Lyon, *Against the Heresies*, Book III, 3, 2.

CHAPTER FIVE

[1] See *Christus Dominus,* #11–14 and *Lumen gentium,* ch. 3.

[2] Klaus Schatz, *Papal Primacy: From Its Origins to the Present* (Collegeville: The Liturgical Press, 1996) 167–68.

[3] Vatican I, *Pastor Aeternus,* in *Decrees of the Ecumenical Councils,* Norman Tanner, ed. (Washington, D.C.: Georgetown University Press, 1990) II: 816.

[4] Although this did not appear in the council's constitution, this assumption was made explicit by Bishop Gasser, the official spokesperson for the commission charged with drafting and amending the council document.

[5] Francis A. Sullivan, s.j., *Creative Fidelity: Weighing and Interpreting Documents of the Magisterium* (New York: Paulist, 1996) 86.

CHAPTER SIX

[1] "Challenge of Peace," #10.

CHAPTER SEVEN

[1] For this treatment of the *sensus fidei,* see Ormond Rush, "*Sensus Fidei*: Faith "Making Sense" of Revelation," *Theological Studies* 62 (June, 2001) 231–61.

[2] John Henry Newman, *On Consulting the Faithful in Matters of Doctrine* (1859; reprint, Kansas City: Sheed & Ward, 1961).

[3] Ibid., 163.

[4] St. Cyprian of Carthage, *Epistle,* 74, 10.

[5] Congregation for the Clergy, *General Directory for Catechesis* (Washington, D.C.: u.s.c.c., 1997) #78.

[6] J-M.R. Tillard, "Tradition, Reception," in *The Quadrilog. Tradition and the Future of Ecumenism* (Collegeville: The Liturgical Press, 1994) 328–43 at 336.

[7] The Anglican-Roman Catholic Dialogue (arcic II), "The Gift of Authority," *Origins* 29 (May 27, 1999) #s 24–25.

CHAPTER EIGHT

[1] In what follows I am adapting Francis Sullivan's helpful treatment of the dynamics of internal assent in *Magisterium: Teaching Authority in the Church* (New York: Paulist, 1983) 162–66.

[2] S.v., "Epikeia," *HarperCollins Encyclopedia of Catholicism* (San Francisco, HarperCollins, 1995).

[3] *Acta Synodalia,* IV/6, 769, as quoted in Sullivan, *Magisterium,* 169.

CHAPTER NINE

[1] The English translation of this document can be found in *Readings in Moral Theology No. 3,* Charles E. Curran and Richard A. McCormick, eds. (New York: Paulist, 1982) 151–70.

2 For an analysis of this document see Francis A. Sullivan, *Magisterium: Teaching Authority in the Catholic Church* (New York: Paulist, 1983) 192–93.

3 N.C.C.B., *Doctrinal Responsibilities: Approaches to Promoting Cooperation and Resolving Misunderstandings between Bishops and Theologians* (Washington, D.C.: U.S.C.C., 1989).

4 Congregation for the Doctrine of the Faith, "Instruction on the Ecclesial Vocation of the Theologian," *Origins* 20 (July 5, 1990) 117–26.

5 See *Theses*, 2 & 3; CDF Instruction, #s 4 & 5; N.C.C.B., *Doctrinal Responsibilities*, 3.

6 Cardinal Joseph Ratzinger, "Theology is not Private Idea of Theologian," *L'Osservatore Romano* [English ed.] 27 (July 2, 1990) 5.

7 Ibid.

8 CDF, "Instruction on the Ecclesial Vocation of the Theologian," #6.

9 *Theses*, 8.2. See also CDF, "Instruction. . . ," #9; N.C.C.B., *Doctrinal Responsibilities*, 7.

10 CDF, "Instruction on the Ecclesial Vocation of the Theologian," #30.

11 Francis A. Sullivan, "Magisterium," *Dictionary of Fundamental Theology*, René Latourelle and Rino Fisichella, eds. (New York: Crossroad, 1994) 616.

INDEX

apostolicity
    of the canon, 34
    of the faith, 42, 43, 46–50, 59,
        68, 82–83, 111, 113, 116–17,
        140–41
    of office, 34, 58–59, 63–64, 111
Apostolos suos, 79, 86
authority. *See also* Bible; magisterium;
    bishops.
    as relational, 37–38, 146–47

Bible. *See also* inspiration, biblical;
    inerrancy, biblical.
    authority of, 30, 36–38
    and New Testament, 33–35
    and Old Testament, 31–33
    Vulgate (*see also* Jerome, Saint),
        29, 38
bishop of Rome. *See* Papacy.
bishops. *See also* collegiality;
    magisterium; *sensus fidei;*
    reception, ecclesial
    exercise of teaching office.
    assisted by the faithful, 116–17
    assisted by the Holy Spirit, 64–65
    assisted by human resources, 65–66
    in early church, 63–64
    as *iudex fidei,* 59
    and *Lumen Gentium,* 58–59
    in relation to the laity, 62–63

in relation to local church, 63–64
    as chief catechist, 76
relationship to papacy, 59–60
responsibilities of, 68–69
as *testis fidei,* 59
as vicars of Christ, 59, 63

canon
    definition of, 31
    feminist critique of, 39
    Judaic, 31–32, 33
    New Testament, 33–35
    Old Testament, 31–33
canon law
    on definitive doctrine, 102
    and ecclesial reception, 113–14
    on infallibility, 85–86
    on *recognitio,* 87
canonicity
    criteria for, 34
    and inspiration, 35–36
Christus Dominus, 76–78
Church
    as a communion of churches, 67–68,
        71
    as a community of dialogue and
        discernment, 117–18
    as sacrament of salvation, 58
college of bishops. *See also* bishops;
    magisterium.

role of the faithful in prophetic
ministry, 108
sensus fidei, 44, 111
on the teaching office of the bishop,
76

magisterium. See also *sensus fidei*;
consensus fidelium.
assisted by the Holy Spirit, 64–65
extraordinary, 75, 81–84
ordinary
exercised by Bishop of Rome,
79–81
exercised by individual bishops,
76–77
exercised in synods and episcopal
conferences, 77–79
ordinary, universal, 75, 84–85, 88
origination of term, 60
in relation to all the faithful, 108,
116–17
in relation to theologians
in the teaching of Vatican II,
136–38
prior to Vatican II, 135–36
Vatican II on, 6
mandatum, 144–45

New Testament
canonicity of, criteria for, 34
origin thereof, 33–35
on revelation, 4

Old Testament
development of, 31–32
on revelation, 4
Orthodox Christianity
and canonicity, 34

papacy
bishop of Rome, 70
documents of
apostolic exhortation, 80
apostolic letter, 80

encyclical letter, 79–80
occasional papal address, 80
exercise of infallibility, 82, 83–84
criteria for, 83–84
instances of, 84
ordinary magisterium of, 79–81
in relation to college of bishops,
70–71
in service to the churches, 71
pneumatology, 107
pope. *See* papacy.
Providentissimus Deus, 21

reception, ecclesial. See also *consensus
fidelium.*
in early Church, 113
juridical view of, 113–14
post Vatican II (*communion*) model,
114–17
role of theologians in, 139–40
responsibility, pastoral
guidance on church teaching,
130–31
presentation of church teaching
as binding, 129–30
comprehensive and sympathetic,
128–29
revelation, divine. See also *Dei Verbum*;
dogma.
as encountered in community, 110
as found in Scripture, 4
and human experience, 9–10
outside Judeo-Christian tradition,
10–11
propositional view of, 3, 6, 9, 17,
25, 44, 90
as related to teaching authority,
135
symbolic, 8
trinitarian view of, 3, 5, 10
two-source theory, 41, 42, 43
unity of, 91
Rome, church of
authority of, 69–70